THE NATURE
OF MORALITY

THE NATURE OF MORALITY

Arnold W. Green

UNIVERSITY
PRESS OF
AMERICA

Lanham • New York • London

Copyright © 1994 by
University Press of America,® Inc.
4720 Boston Way
Lanham, Maryland 20706

3 Henrietta Street
London WC2E 8LU England

All rights reserved
Printed in the United States of America
British Cataloging in Publication Information Available

Library of Congress Cataloging-in-Publication Data
Green, Arnold W.
The nature of morality / Arnold W. Green.
p.   cm.
Includes index.
1. Ethics. 2. Family. 3. Religion. 4. Social classes. 5. United
States—Moral conditions.   I. Title.
BJ1031.G744   1993   170—dc20   93-2205 CIP

ISBN 0-8191-9209-0 (cloth : alk. paper)
ISBN 0-8191-9210-4 (pbk. : alk. paper)

BJ
1031
.G744
1993

 TM   The paper used in this publication meets the minimum requirements of
American National Standard for Information Sciences—Permanence
of Paper for Printed Library Materials, ANSI Z39.48–1984.

CONTENTS

Preface	vii
CHAPTER 1: PERCEPTION AND IDEOLOGY	1
Stereotyping	2
Organized Perception	12
The Symbolic Interactionists	16
Exclusion-Inclusion	24
CHAPTER 2: SELF AND FAMILY	27
The Child Becomes Human	27
Marriage	33
Feminism and Idealization	37
Love and Trust	46
CHAPTER 3: RELATIVISM AND THE FAMILY INSTITUTION	51
Relativism	51
Margaret Mead	55
The Family as Institution	63
Family Rewards	67
Time and Distraction	75
CHAPTER 4: RELIGION AS VITAL FORCE	83
Religion and Social Class	84
Religion and Morality	88
The Social Issues	95
Modern Gnosticism	105

Contents

CHAPTER 5: SOCIAL CLASS AND PREJUDICE — 113
   Snobbery and Higher Education — 113
   The Nature of Prejudice — 123
   Racial and Ethnic Prejudice — 128
   Inevitability of Prejudice — 154

Index — 161

PREFACE

An alternative title for this essay might be *Morality Equals Family, Religion, and Social Class*. All parts of the equation, in about the last three decades and with mounting crescendo, have come under determined attack by ideologues. Militants in the academy, the public school, the print and electronic media, the law, and especially the bureaucracies and seminaries of the established churches, have laid a path of destruction through traditional beliefs that shows no sign of being curbed. Disaffection has become sanctified. Still, part of the current difficulty is an old one, the persisting failure of communication in civilization.

Difficult at any time, communication became impossible at the ideological extremes of progressivism (loyalty to the distant and abstract) and traditionalism (emphasis upon the near and the particular). Stereotyping thus became practiced more, not less, and fixed pictures in the mind came to dominate attention while they were being denounced. With an egalitarian bias the new elite inveighed against elitism, was not so much concerned to seize power as to achieve a pose of ideational superiority. Such a posture accompanied an invocation of social engineering, that is, an extension of direct government control. Other people might otherwise refuse to behave as they should.

The resulting intensified social struggle is most accurately portrayed in our court system, where the traditional sense of responsibility confronts a progressive determination to expand such explanations of immoral behavior as victimization and underlying basic causes. The social workers, who control juvenile courts, have been indoctrinated by "situational ethics" and "cognitive moral development" so that they avoid questions of right and wrong: what may be understandable for one person in one situation may not at all apply to another person in a different situation. But since the fixing of responsibility is an inevitable human quest, the conclusion follows that the non-criminal must be held responsible for crime. Blaming the non-criminal ("society") has become fashionable among those charged with applying legal proceedings to adults as well. Such a violent departure from reality represents a failure of collective will, of shared purpose.

The reality of progressivism-traditionalism at the same time is a continuum, so that extremes of opinion are to be found only at the far end of each range. Still, the separation between "us" and "them" persists across each range, because perceptions inevitably define outsiders. This point was made by all the symbolic interactionists of the 20th century, Charles Horton Cooley in particular. Much less convincing was his sharing with the others a vision of history as ineluctably moving toward enlightened democracy. These people also ignored the glaring fact of self-absorption, and the resulting inevitability of suppression and repression when perceived interests clash. All of them, as did previous philosophers, mistakenly located order in the collectivity instead of the individual's voluntary acts of repression.

Human order needs repression, the voluntary control of contrary impulses. This control is traceable to the rules accepted through identification within close and continuous association with those adults who have been trained in their own turn to accept responsibility, and to reject the temptations of individuated hedonism which, within some range of tolerance, must be suppressed from the outside. When repression dominates choice, marriage comes to have a high priority, a circumstance enforced by an idealization of female by male, based upon a belief in her superior restraint. Feminism has rejected that idealization, as well as the evidence that all women are not represented by militant feminists, who express a preference for sex, without consequences or responsibility, over mutual trust.

Militant feminists only exaggerate the dominant mode of modern thought—relativism—in which facts exist solely because they reflect a specific history, of a person or a collectivity. Oddly enough, such a claim of value neutrality accompanies a conviction that other peoples, especially the uncivilized, are somehow correct in the judgments of ourselves imputed to them. Margaret Mead is the most famous contributor to this outlook, although how much she and other individuals accomplished apart from a search by progressives for scientific evidence such as hers is an unanswerable question.

In either event, the family as an institution is the ultimate basis of continuity and morality, and the blessings of that mutual trust are more craved than they are rejected amidst pressures to throw off restraint and live one's own life. The history of the Christian School movement, which has been commonly misunderstood, shows what can be done to combat the sociological factors of industrialism, urbanism, and mobility, which in some quarters have been said to render the family obsolete. The Christian School movement also offers additional presumptive evidence of the intrinsic whole which is religion and morality, and the proper assignment of order to individuals rather than to the collectivity.

Religion, however, has never been mere sweetness and light. Religion embodies exclusion as well as inclusion. And despite the historic connection between class and exploitation, religion is thus akin to social class in affirming standards of consciously superior conduct.

The critical issues of pornography and abortion make totally explicit the theme of exclusion-inclusion, even pornography, which cannot be physically avoided today. The issue also persists in consciousness because of the contradictory attraction-repulsion aroused in constant human nature. Abortion, likewise, is ineradicable, a "problem" that will never be "solved," no more in the future than in the past. But it has become an obsession to traditionalists, who believe that their own basic loyalty to human life has been officially repudiated.

Religious tenets have been weakened as well. The progressive rejection of them, though, has led less to the victory of secularism than to counterfeit religions, in one way or another to Gnosticism, ultimately self-worship, as the concept of God-as-other has been rejected, even within the seminaries and among church bureaucrats. Either way of defining God, the expressed desire to live beyond one's own fingertips remains as imperious a drive as ever. Religion cannot be abandoned; only superstition of one kind or another can substitute for it, as in the "religious" cast of the Enlightenment or the Marxist faith. The modern situation has been complicated by a radical twist to relativism which converts any variant human wish into truth.

What has virtually destroyed the modern university, and stultifies the public schools, is the elaboration of relativism known as egalitarian snobbery, accompanied by its child, political correctness. Horrified rejection of an older snob-

Preface

bery has only demonstrated its necessary place in standards of superior conduct, and the need for as well as inevitability of prejudice. This misunderstood attitude remains ubiquitous, celebrated by the very people who denounce it. The targets may shift identity, true enough, as in the extremely rancorous prejudice aimed at traditionalists in the modern world.

And there is no way to erase such substitutes for social class as the attitudes of various racial and ethnic groups toward one another. They do not believe, as do doctrinaire progressives, in the basic equality (or alikeness) of all groups. The new elite may inveigh against elitism, and stress basic equality, but various ethnic groups neither believe in nor endorse it—as shown by Oriental immigrants, the last British wave of immigration, by American Jews and American blacks.

Illusions of egalitarian harmony also serve the organizationally divided and fractionated purposes of government personnel. Especially do competing politicians feel compelled to manipulate the voter instead of seek out what is called the common good. The led, as well, tend to ignore the possibility that political flattery, while they are being bribed by tax money, might lead to unwanted results. All are actually engaged in the ancient opportunistic struggle, ultimately rooted in human nature, but that struggle must now face the added complication that rules are more contradictory than ever before. A radical increase in non-communication has been one ironic consequence of unleashed claims to literal equality.

1

PERCEPTION AND IDEOLOGY

Ideological opposites do not communicate with one another for they cannot. Ideologies do change in time, mainly because a given conjunction of perceived interests first begins to change. But persuasion has little if anything to do with the matter, since traditionalists (those who live primarily in terms of the near and the particular) and progressives (those who orient themselves in terms of the distant and the abstract) at any given moment talk past one another. At both extremes of these crude ranges, and depending upon which ideology is regnant at the time, only the threat by a militant minority to ruin the reputations and lives of their declared enemies can "persuade."

In the more usual case honest puzzlement affects most of those members of each ideological camp, those who are reasonably free of hatred and the desire to punish. For example, the Dean of the Graduate School at a famous university responded to an editorial charge that "American universities have embraced thought control, political re-education and other basics of totalitarianism" with what was, to her, perfectly obvious: There can be no error in stating that "We are all the progeny of a racist and sexist society." Reminding others about the "realities of sexism" exercises no "thought control over the minds of men and women."

The Nature of Morality

A reminder of the "realities of racism" will hardly enslave students. "On the contrary, as the Western tradition teaches, the truth does set one free." Sadly enough, the truth the Western tradition teaches seems at the other end of the ideological scale to resemble nothing that the Dean finds unexceptionable.

Realities, and facts as well, vary from one mind to another because of the way the mind works. The realities of racism, for the Dean, comprise favorable black images and unfavorable white ones. In recent years more people have come to share her prejudices than in previous eras. Since a given consensus is forever shifting, slowly or quickly, communication is possible only within a narrow band of a given shift. More important, the mind entertains only concrete images, of one entity at a time, even when addressing an abstraction. When images meld together, the composite struggles against dilution, strives to remain one image.

STEREOTYPING

Strangely enough there has been little added to knowledge about stereotyping, except for a greater physiological precision, since Walter Lippmann published his *Public Opinion* in 1922. As is characteristic of modern science, an insistence upon exactitude has sacrificed meaning and significance. Studies of perception have tended to become technical treatises, such as measurement of eye movements when different pictures are flashed upon a screen. Lippmann's insights about the nature of stereotyping have hardly been improved upon.

Stereotyping tunnels perception into a series of fixed yet alternating pictures in the mind, pictures which shape the reality to which we react. Our referents are never entirely

Perception and Ideology

free from our own creation. In this connection Lippmann had at his disposal the work of the early symbolic interactionists, in particular Cooley, who is discussed below.

These pictures in the mind are what clash in the social struggle—albeit unevenly. Although the extreme progressives comprise only a minority, they are strategically located within the division of labor, so that they control the means of public communication. They are much over-represented in the print and electronic media, the universities, among the church officials and the legal profession. Only a climate of shared opinion holds them together, not at all a plot or conspiracy. Like the cited Dean, they are honestly puzzled by a failure of the majority to see the truth, and they have dedicated their lives to instruct and lead the majority.

But the pictures in their minds continue to clash with those held by the majority. The political process is the common focus of attention, where politicians strive to sustain a picture assumed to be already there, or to replace one picture with another deemed more advantageous to themselves. Rarely is public virtue and high purpose invoked, which was the announced goal of the early American constitutionalists, who hoped various self-serving factions would pay heed to it. Lower motives such as envy, power-seeking, insecurity, raw greed and vanity are probably now more often addressed than they were at that time. All modern politicians repeat, over and over again, that the American people are much smarter than the politicians.

Politicians know well that a picture held in most single minds is in varying degree an unstable construct. Shifting about is especially apparent when the verities and prejudices of one generation appear less certain than they did in even the recent past. That is one of the reasons why sudden and massive changes in so-called public opinion, notably in racial and ethnic expression, are impossible to trace. There can be no answer, only a lame explanation about the openness of human nature to change when confronted by a shifting conjunction of perceived effective interests.

A further complication emerges from attitudes held in separate compartments of the mind, those officially enforced and overtly expressed, and those which may lay hidden from the self when they are not challenged by experience. While only one picture can be held in the mind at one time, the picture can switch from that of a winsome, starch-dressed little black girl denied access to a full life by some pot-bellied white sheriff to one of menacing young black toughs crowding the sidewalk. Changes in personal experience affect which kind of picture will crowd to attention, but even changes in experience may leave the matter unaffected. Ideological loyalty does much to control which composite picture more often will dominate attention.

Although added uncertainties are not needed, what is also unknown is what the *direct* influence of certain individuals might be in controlling exactly what pictures in the mind will come to dominate ideology and politics. Are such influential persons more cause of the immediate future than they are the result of a given present? Margaret Mead, for example, was both precipitant and reflection of changing pictures in the mind which followed the intrusion of World War I. At the same time, her career provides a bench mark in the master shift from religious familism to hedonic individuation. On the one hand her personal influence was unmistakable, on the other she provided scientific answers that the progressives of the early twenties were already seeking. These matters are discussed more fully below, in Chapter 3.

Perception and Ideology

The Fallacy of Contextual Choice

Even experts commit the psychologist's error, fail to prove their assumption that one's own experience of life can be relied upon to understand how other people are motivated, especially what pictures must preside in the minds of others. That particular error can be complicated by the fallacy of contextual choice. All anthropologists insist upon a recognition of cultural integration, but from time to time some of them commit the fallacy by insisting that "we" can select out of any collective whole an alien practice and easily confer it upon others or even adopt one for ourselves.

The idea will not work and the practice makes for bungling. Such deliberate efforts surely produce results, but mostly unwanted ones. Thus the "freedom" and "independence" which accompanied highly particular economic and political developments in the West brought chaos and starvation once they were imposed upon those artificially constructed nations of Africa, which remain based upon tribal organization and a feudal economy.

The fallacy of contextual choice can also involve one people within their own history. The belief that a perception of the world which arose under a restricted set of conditions can at a later time be revived intact is an error, for not only has that perception inevitably changed but so also has changed the background in which the perception emerged. In this connection the President's Committee on Juvenile Delinquency and Youth Crime once underwrote local plans to furnish rafts that would drift groups of supervised teenagers down the Mississippi.

Modern laws to reinstate the past cannot make sovereign a morality which is maintained only by enclaves continuously threatened with invasion. Morning prayers in public schools, for example, were once an expression, not a cause, of strong community religious sentiment. If the movement to reinstate what the Supreme Court has frowned upon should succeed through improbable magic, progressives would have little to fear. On the other hand, if morning prayers in public schools *could* be reinstituted, the opposition to this and a range of other issues would be in concurrent retreat. In such a case morning prayers would once again become an expression of united public sentiment.

Finally, we are now under extreme pressure to exaggerate any concern "we" may have for others. Huxley once said that anyone can become reconciled to someone else's asthma. Beyond self and the circle of the personally known, concern dribbles off from class and ethnic and religious identification to a nod of recognition for the common humanity of those who live far away—unless they can serve as a symbolic prop to self-esteem.

Only when one is granted the opportunity to announce the purity of his own intention among like-minded others is there any point in embracing some cause or other designed to rescue faceless people at a distance. When Idi Amin's troopers in Uganda were murdering Asians and blacks, not to control the ones allowed to live but simply to eliminate those capriciously chosen for death, there was no popular outcry in America. What point could have been scored?

Stereotyping in the Courts

Nowhere was stereotyping more blatant, and intransigent, than in the criminal justice system of late 20th century. On one side traditionalists insisted upon personal respon-

Perception and Ideology

sibility, on the other progressives rarely saw anything other than underlying causes and victimization. But it was only at the extreme end of the progressive range that the ideological assault on the traditionalist's morality engaged an army wearing distinctive uniforms.

Social workers, for example, were more driven than driving, at least in the lower ranks. For the most part dedicated, idealistic, humanitarian people, they felt impelled to help others. One of their assignments, to rehabilitate juvenile delinquents, at one time would have been clear enough, but later there was nothing to return delinquents to. The habits and goals of respectability became quaint to social workers, if not personally offensive. In the textbooks they had studied the term "middle-class morality" was one of opprobrium.

Their teachers, graduates of the most prestigious educational institutions, laid stress upon avoiding what they called the indoctrination of values in favor of "cognitive moral development." The basic idea echoed Rousseau: avoid imposing standards of any kind and allow the subject to find his own way, because standards are a matter of choice. They declared that what is right for one person may not be right for another. They were unprepared to try to dissuade young thugs from the pleasures of the moment, to defer gratification and to apply means to some future goal. And in effect they settled whatever case they presented to a local judge who lacked their degrees and who, with a heavy docket of cases, invariably accepted the expert's judgment on the disposition of the given case.

For the social worker, especially the young one with recent training, steering protected charges away from the ecstatic moment would have seemed like going against the tide, selling out to the squares. Thus it was that while the more sophisticated social workers avoided the exculpatory rhetoric of victimhood, they still confirmed their charges in what they were and already did. They continued to reinforce the idea that "society" and not the individual is responsible for his own conduct.

But if the fallacy of misplaced concreteness is to be avoided, a society comprises all of the people associated by politically-defined territory. These people are divisible into those who commit crime and those who do not commit crime. If the criminals are not responsible for crime, then the law-abiding people must be held responsible for crime.

Although the simplicity of that proposition is never introduced in court, it lies beneath arguments often advanced by defense attorneys when they declare that society made him (increasingly her) do it. Still, here as elsewhere, the only sensorium is the individual brain, and there is no procedural way that an entity called society can be charged with guilt; conversely, no such entity can take action addressed to a single point. At the moment of encounter no man finds an abstraction, only himself or others of his own kind.

But in the battle to expand criminal rights, more people than social workers and defense attorneys veered close to blaming the non-criminal. More people came to be offended by respectability. Some of them either attacked it as in the media treatment of Christianity, or attempted further to undermine it as in the agenda of trendy clergymen. The various ways in which rules of any kind throughout history have remained inconsistent, contradictory, and unfair, became a justification for denouncing the abstraction called society, while traditionalists complained that the law was enforced only against those who obeyed it.

The rectitude of those individuals who then as always

maintained order, however, deserves little commendation. Neither saints nor especially "good" people, they were merely those who to their own satisfaction in their overt conduct resolved whatever contradictions they faced. They were no superior breed, although possibly they were somewhat less guilty of hypocrisy than were their opponents. In either event, their attempts to live orderly lives were much more penalized than in previous eras.

Real Reality?

The distinction between reality and perception fails to trouble the politician, only the men of thought. Does perception, the image of reality, exhaust reality? An apparently increasing number of intellectuals now think that what we envision and what is out there cannot be separated. Still, in the world even philosophers must inhabit, there is a relative possibility of real reality in one case compared with another.

Any possibility of empirical verification, for example, advances with concrete manifestation and recedes when abstraction expands, as in the image of America held in late 20th century. Some people perceived the American Leviathan as a beached whale or sick giant; others perceived evil incarnate, the source of all malignancy in the world; and still others, the common people for the most part, remained simply patriotic. There was no referent for "America" except for highly variant images of it.

Perceived images of reality also play a complex role in the rewriting of history. There is first the matter of who shall be blamed, and who shall be vindicated, through identification with those vindicated. Once a public image of hero (or heroic victim) has been created by extensive propaganda and pathos manipulation, any evidence which might question established heroism on one side, villainy on the other, encounters either apathy or resistance.

Even people whose interests and prejudices might be served by such evidence can find it somehow unsuitable. It does not fit the image which, perhaps reluctantly in some cases, they have come to accept. Thus military General S. L. A. Marshall persuaded very few with his evidence that the Indian wars on the Great Plains were savagely fought on both sides, with no master plan of genocide, and perhaps he convinced none with his finding that by deliberate conspiracy Black Fox and other Sioux fired the first shots at—the site is horrendously inappropriate—Wounded Knee.

Social reality, then, is an insecure combination of what is "objectively" out there and shifting images of what is assumed to be out there. In a radical view, a view apparently gaining intellectual acceptance, reality is entirely subjective. Professor Kenneth E. Boulding has insisted in his *The Image* (University of Michigan, 1961) that "facts do not exist for any organism, organization, or even scientist" (pages 11–12). There are only messages, which filter through changeable value systems. Messages which cannot be fitted into images (or perceptions) already held are usually ignored; messages which reinforce an image already held are eagerly sought.

In Boulding's view, scientists are no less prone to folly than ordinary clay. A scientist's frame of reference is a "subjective knowledge structure," as much a value to be defended as it is a means to interpret data. No orthodox psychologist, for example, would ever welcome evidence which might serve to substantiate the claims of ESP practitioners, any more than an advocate of ESP would welcome counterevidence.

Perception and Ideology

Evidence may very well be found only on shifting sand, but there are some circumstances which at least foster more agreement about what is, or happened, than do other circumstances. The Wounded Knee episode is hopeless. What happened there is so widely accepted that General Marshall's attempt to prove what *really* happened was bound to fail. On the other hand, there are cases where a given record is so extensive that distortion of it is thwarted.

Even when ideology rules supreme, as in the progressive-traditionalist controversy over proper interpretation of the Bible, the facts—in this instance what has been written and come down to us—are so widely known, mirrored in so many different languages, that, for example, the attempt to prove that St. Paul really intended to display a benign attitude toward homosexuality can hardly survive indefinitely. Boulding's assertion about the sovereignty of images at least has only uneven and modifiable application. History may be in constant process of being rewritten, but there are limits to what transitory fads can do to change it at will.

Again, evidence is more readily acknowledged in matters of applied technology than in those where ideology rules. Man pursues his own perceived material and ideal interests, and he now, formerly, and forever is ruled by emotion, so he is most easily persuaded to accept evidence in those cases where his emotions are not involved. Perception can occur more accurately when evidence least affects the self and its affiliations.

Thus research on the number of Toyotas imported last year is not likely to excite a denial of stated fact, however unpleasant to an auditor that fact might be. But an attempt by *Consumer Reports* to settle whether a Toyota or a Buick performs better on the road *will* provoke denials to such claimed "facts," because in this case politics and ideology have a part to play, however indirect—possibly a reminder that a relative's job is threatened, a prod to someone else's war memories, perhaps anger at Japanese government subsidies for exporters or anger about reputed sloppy job performance in Detroit.

The only issues free of possible ideological taint are technological ones—narrowly considered. Whether to add fluorides to public water supplies is inescapably an ideological question, how fluorides have been manufactured is not. Only questions about applied technology can virtually ignore refractory human beings. That is why "we" are able to produce efficient weapons but are unable to confer peace.

There is one way that evidence about what is out there is forced into shared recognition, and at the very core of self at that. Perception of one's own self is in part corrected by the inferred judgments of others, however hard the lesson that one's own sense of importance is not shared. Anyone who persists in grossly overestimating his own importance is, in the popular outlook, "crazy," for empirical evidence to back such a claim is lacking. The hard consequences are real enough.

ORGANIZED PERCEPTION

Progressivism, like traditionalism, is an organized way of perceiving the world and self within it. Not everyone, especially among the common people, performs such a creative act with consistency and elaboration. Instead such people adapt to their immediate world with habit, with received folk wisdom, and show little desire either to improve distant others or to quarrel with those who try.

But the common people are not nearly the majority they

Perception and Ideology

once were. For one thing they must ignore their public-school education, which is designed to foster progressive opinions. Those who either resist or fail to absorb that experience become non-ideological traditionalists—perhaps illogically, traditionalism is as much a matter of becoming as being. In either case, progressives and ideological traditionalists feel equal pressure to adopt a consistent, resistive, organized view of the world. That is one reason why a persisting hope in rational argument to dissuade others from their obviously foolish opinions remains a will-o'-the-wisp throughout time.

Whether for common people or sophisticates, the world is viewed through pictures in the mind which can ignore argument or even evidence. Sophisticates on either side can only hallucinate about settling once and for all the quarrels separating them. When, for example, World Communism, at least in temporary appearance, collapsed, some Americans declared victory because their uncompromising insistence upon unilateral disarmament ("Arms Are For Holding") finally had exerted persuasion abroad if not at home. Other Americans, with like absolute conviction, insisted that only American rearmament had priced the Communists out of the war market.

What actually may happen in national as well as international matters is screened by the given fixed position. When the late Senator Hubert Humphrey was publicly challenged by the patent failure of all of the Great Society programs, he snapped back that "we" had refused to appropriate enough money for them. There will be no change of heart through conversion. One side will continue to stress the sanctity of intention, the other the limits of possibility.

We fail to communicate, even in the declared area of public concern. Technological improvements confer no means to do so. The possibilities of misunderstanding are compounded, so that TV and radio "talk shows" either go nowhere or feature shouting matches designed to provide amusement.

In this and similar discussions no one is dissuaded. What explicitly lends an air of unreality to all confrontations between ideological traditionalists and progressives, are the unstated assumptions which carry the separate arguments. In any argument over the sexual attitudes and practices of the young, for example, whether on the floor of the Senate or in the corner bar, one side assumes as perfectly obvious that the future of Western civilization rests with restraint and discipline, the other that if only freedom and liberty were encouraged, the world would become a better place.

The Separation Persists

The unresolved debate has been going on for centuries. Perhaps the argument between those who view a universal human nature as being immutable, and those who see human potential as being limitless, is an inevitable accompaniment of civilization. Progressives have always tended to believe that evil is curable, while their opponents trace evil to a universal propensity which requires control, either from within or without. In this view man is not perfectible but permanently flawed, as the Bible affirms, so that no special causes for crime need be sought. Those who believe on the other hand that evil is curable are naturally enough horrified by punishment and recoil from it. They look upon decency as the natural condition, not something which must be taught. Closely allied with this attitude is an egalitarian bias which rules progressive thought, so that

Perception and Ideology

known inequities are intolerable, whereas for traditionalists individual rewards should reflect worth as closely as possible.

Distinctive attitudes toward the common people are critical for distinguishing traditionalists from progressives. The first is one of tolerance, to let others do what they want within the constraints of law. Progressives, on the other hand, tend to regard common people as in constant need of improvement, as misguided without direction and control by an elite, by a "we." Power, as control, is a precious thing for those who share the progressive outlook, because they believe that a choice to correct benighted others on a massive scale forever awaits the enlightened.

Separation between traditionalists and progressives has persisted, even though the balance of power between them has shifted from time to time, as the near and the particular or the distant and the abstract temporarily tip the scales. Traditionalist and progressive, however, are rarely embodied in pure form. With only a short distance from the ideological extremes, opinions on particular issues tend to blur. No dichotomy which is also a continuum will ever entirely separate sheep from goats. Only at the extreme of each ideological range, for example, is found an obsession about what the future should be.

But however much the categories may overlap, perceptions which are organized are always organized against outsiders. No ideology exists without such meat to feed upon. True, the we-and-they confrontation can and does operate without ideology, although less and less so in late 20th century. At century's start Cooley, the coiner of in-group vs. out-group, could envision a world where people strove for visible objects, not control of images, the pictures in the minds of others. He could thus regard strife

The Nature of Morality

benignly, as something an unfolding democracy which scorned ideology would soften. Basically, however, Cooley remains correct: mind is organized in terms of inclusion and exclusion. Although he was only one of several symbolic interactionists, his conceptual scheme forced him to deal more directly with this issue than did any of the others.

THE SYMBOLIC INTERACTIONISTS

The first half of the 20th century witnessed a radical departure from the prevailing scientism through a new way of looking at behavior—as the point of view of the subject and what he is trying to do. An object to others, even to himself, *he* nevertheless initiates, acts as well as is acted upon. Hereditary and conditioning factors are not dismissed; they are merely assumed in order to focus upon the emergent self, the conscious agent who applies means to some *projected* end he has in view. Whatever the end-result might be lies outside theoretical attention.

The symbolic interactionists said in common that people orient themselves not toward events and others but toward their own conceptions—or perceptions—of events and others. An intricate web of like and contested meanings thus becomes the basic stuff of man in his world. This common approach to reality was taken by all the great sociological theorists in their own different terms. Thus Max Weber promoted the "sociology of understanding," while Charles H. Cooley referred to society as "a relation among personal ideas." W. I. Thomas said that "a situation defined as real is real in its consequences," and proper study focuses upon those definitions, not upon a reality imposed by the investigator. Talcott Parsons singled out "the point of view of the actor" as critical and Robert M.

MacIver used the actor's "dynamic assessment," of groups as well as individuals, in exactly the same way.

Charles Horton Cooley (1864–1929), like many another writer was prone to make sweeping statements, and then modify them as need arose. He will be remembered, however, not for imputed lapses but for three great coinages. First, this most radical of the symbolic interactionists differentiated between primary and secondary groups. On the one hand are groups which hold people closely together in organic relationships, such as a family or small village. On the other are groups which are of relative indifference to the given person, because of their size, dispersal, and heterogeneity. Still, the "we-feeling" engendered in primary groups—and here is a small lapse—exerts a predominance that, in echo of Goethe and Emerson, will ensure a pleasing whole, will counteract the disjointive effects of secondary groups, so that men will become almost literally one body. Each person, Cooley moralized in his *Human Nature and the Social Order* (Scribners, 1922), "contributes something to the common life that no one else can . . ." (page 35).

Cooley's second neologism was what made him famous: the looking-glass self. By way of the looking-glass, self and social almost fuse. Our ideas, loyalties, attitudes, and points of view derive from others. Within intimate social relations we surmise how we are regarded at the moment by others, how others view our appearance and action, and how they interpret our vocal responses. Then we imagine what their judgment is of what we infer they experience. Finally, we react to our imagination of their judgment, are pleased or downcast, flattered or dejected. In brief, we derive our self-conception from others. We live in the eyes of others, and "society" has its locus in individual minds.

The Nature of Morality

Only by becoming an object to self through the inferred judgments of close others does moral behavior become possible, possible but not inevitable. For what follows next Cooley is not responsible: morality or lack of it depends primarily upon the *character* of that symbolic communication all infants and small children enter upon. In some cases, not all, high standards are transmitted along with the universal and slow introjection of others. Expectations of self, whether high or low, tend to follow expectations of introjected others. Moral behavior, which is principled self-restriction of impulse accepted before temptation or opportunity arises, in other words, does not inevitably result from every emergence of self. On this point Cooley, with his democratic bias, was equivocal.

There are other dimensions in the operation of the looking-glass. Of remote villagers in early 17th-century England it has been said that they were too much concerned about small matters to adopt another's point of view. Cooley modified his central contribution in a similar way: "People differ much in the vividness of their imaginative sociability. The more simple, concrete, dramatic, their habit of mind is, the more their thinking is carried on in terms of actual conversation with a visible and audible interlocutor" (page 95).

George Herbert Mead, another symbolic interactionist, was disturbed by Cooley's notion that society is located in the minds of individuals. There must be something more that is objectively there, which he located in the "generalized other," an embodiment of the point of view of the entire community. That sum total is introjected in what Mead called a conversation of gestures, by means of which individuals, and individual differences, if anything become more vague than in Cooley's less rigorous formulations. The self becomes almost indistinguishable from its own environment, which led one of Mead's critics, T. V. Smith, to offer the advice that George might keep his eye on the ball, not roving about the stadium.

The looking-glass survived Mead's doubts, but was damaged by Cooley's failure to conceive of it as a double image. Morality, like any other trait or attitude, derives from others, yet as the self emerges it no longer, as in the case of the infant or small child, reflects directly the point of view of the other. Especially in a highly-differentiated social world does discrimination arise in accepting the inferred judgments of the general run of people. To the extent that the self becomes firmly structured—and here individual differences of considerable magnitude must be allowed, as well as the strain introduced by compulsive egalitarianism—resistance develops to the evaluation of some persons, never all, with whom the self interacts.

Habitual aggressiveness is a trait not readily modified when a person who has it finds himself in the company of those who show distaste for such behavior. And attitudes arising out of traits, such as a love for one's own musical talent, can promote a conscious rejection of most inferred-other judgments. The accomplished pianist, if he is more than a celebrity, tends to seek out his own kind, and may live in an isolated world of musicians, composers, and critics. How he may be "reflected" by politicians and businessmen could be of no concern to him; most politicians and businessmen would heartily reciprocate.

Cooley's failure to view the looking-glass as a double image led him to underestimate the extent of self-absorption. Each emergent self converts what comes to it from the outside into an image of itself playing the main role in the human drama. Some people are selfish, others not, but that distinction does not affect self-absorption. Not even a saint can avoid whatever his own defined private and peculiar good may be.

The looking glass as double image can be used to explain why the public self differs, albeit in varying degree, from the private self. Browning thanked God he had two soul sides, one to show the woman he loved, the other to face the world with. The private self can be much more hidden than that. In a classless world with so many individuated strivers, a nimble ability to supply the inferred responses that will advantage self or organization has become highly prized, although that ability also promotes difficulty in separating what is acceptable from what is phony.

The looking-glass self was Cooley's most famous contribution, but his third major coinage is for the moment of major concern, in-group vs. out-group, despite the fact that any awareness of kinship between them has become virtually inadmissible. That inclusion inevitably accompanies exclusion as a proposition has become ideologically unacceptable. The distinction is, nevertheless, universally experienced in time and space: the structure of even intimate primary groups requires an exclusion of others from a precious relationship—from a friendship, a marriage, or a family. Among secondary groups, unlike primary or face-to-face groups, there is always *conscious* opposition to the outside, along a sliding scale, from organized church bodies to nations. Morale and cohesiveness are always strengthened within a country by a violent opposition to an outside counterpart, as in the temporary moratorium on secondary-group internal conflict during wartime.

Cooley may have emphasized exclusion as well as inclusion in his in-group vs. out-group formation, but he, like the other symbolic interactionists, glossed over the inevitable place of conflict in social life, the clash of interests,

Perception and Ideology

the patent lack of harmony, the awareness that when the self becomes an object to itself that the object still has fish of its own to fry. There is no provision made for the isolated self, with its vanity and drive to dominate. There is, for the symbolic interactionist, no Sinbad the Sailor protesting "I am a stranger here, and not subject to your customs."

The concealed bias of the symbolic interactionists also includes some assumptions about democracy, especially the notion that continued association must lead to only one conclusion. For Mead, the individual is guided aright by what is out there, and the rules do not come to him as a series of contradictions. For Cooley, the we-feeling generated within small primary groups expands to resolve all contradictions within an encompassing, harmonious whole. Even though "hard-working people" should (with some condescension) be permitted to organize as unions, they will choose their political leaders shrewdly because "democracy is not the rule of an irresponsible mob." The "dominant moral thought of a group," Cooley said, sets the standards from which only "a degenerate" departs (page 402). The common bias of these men included a belief in the drift of history toward an enlightened democratic world. This focus upon men's interpretation of their world as the touchstone of desired social action led to exaggeration of the freedom in which they move, implied some kind of equality in bringing about social change. But while all men do relate to their world by means of, say, the dynamic assessment, each assessment differs from others in the extent of temptation to take action. Any individual's assessment is made within a shifting range of restriction, which includes suppression and manipulation. In short, not all dynamic assessments are equally effective, no matter what the political system.

The Nature of Morality

Time was drawing short for Mead, Cooley, and all the other symbolic interactionists, Parsons included, with his ultimate values uniting total populations. What were for Mead the sharp outlines of the generalized other became hazier, and the we-feeling of the shared community, even when Cooley wrote, was not what it had been. In late 20th century there were two social types who were keen adepts at understanding the other's point of view, conmen and politicians. These people were expert manipulators who lived in a world of sheer calculation. The looking glass fails to ensure morality.

The gaseous bloat of abstraction plainly drifts along the landscape of symbolic interactionism. According to Cooley, the test of "right, freedom, progress" is the "instructed conscience." If this means anything, it is tautological. And even the instructed conscience does not predictably result in the moral individual.

The moral person is made possible by a self-conception—produced in large measure by the looking-glass—which is elevated to the most valuable of personal possessions. Morality then becomes much more than obedience to a set of rules, although rules are initially essential. The moral person rejects at least some opportunities to aggrandize self because of an overriding need to live with self. It is but a seeming contradiction that the moral person can emerge only from the self-denials specified in conventional morality and, ultimately, in religion, and at the same time that everyone, moral or vicious—with the possible exception of psychopaths or Cooley's degenerates—incorporates a self dependent upon those with whom he closely associates.

Cooley's insights fortunately surpassed his own suasive purpose. That purpose was made clear by his discussion of "personal degeneracy." In the 1902 version of his main work, a degenerate is someone who rejects the moral standards of the group. In the 1922 version, the threat of German militarism having intervened, the degenerate standards of a group may instigate personal degenerate behavior for which no "intrinsic inferiority" of the individual should be assumed.

Cooley and the others still proved their main point: people are moved, and behave, not in terms of "facts" but instead by how they interpret those facts to be. Not facts, but how the selective imagination assesses them, plays the main role in determining what will happen in the social struggle. Facts are not out there whether or not discovered; they are always dependent upon both players and observer. And so long as relativism continues to dominate interpretation, facts will so remain.

Their main point proven, Cooley and his fellow practitioners at the same time opened a methodological can of worms. With all the unenumerated hereditary and conditioning factors held in abeyance, how reduce to a science the most careful inferences about mental states revealed in action? Such inferences about others' interpretations require a subtle and partly artistic process of sympathetic reconstruction. The observer reconstructs in his own mind how stimuli were experienced and what decision and what goal were formed in consequence. Such a task is a hazardous one, and it can never become accepted as scientific procedure. The process of sympathetic reconstruction cannot be replicated or even taught.

Sympathetic reconstruction is only one part of a permanent methodological dilemma. What is most true about individual and collective behavior can least be demonstrated with exactitude. The modern stress upon methodological precision has fostered reductionism, for example, the reduction of perception to a measure of eye-movements.

EXCLUSION-INCLUSION

Cooley's work on in-group vs. out-group was for present purposes his main contribution. Inescapably the mind organizes the world around it in terms of inclusion and exclusion, we and those others. Prejudice is thus ineradicable. An historical target may lose such a dubious distinction, only to be later reinstated. Alternatively, a massive shifting of targets can occur.

There has been no waning of prejudice in recent years. Racial and ethnic prejudice in overt expression may have become totally inadmissible, but at the same time prejudice against all conventional people, especially traditionalists, came to exceed all forms of dismissal and rejection that had gone before. The case could hardly be otherwise. There is no way to eliminate prejudice because pre-judgment is a universal and ineradicable expression of human consciousness. A tremendous upsurge of claims to superiority by all erstwhile conventional targets of prejudice, for example, accompanied the trend toward inadmissibility of overt prejudice against them.

Another aspect of exclusion-inclusion has generally gone unacknowledged. Social class, at the present time virtually destroyed in America, has always presented a Janus face. On one side snobbery, exploitation, and well-controlled expressions of compassion for those without privilege. On the other, standards of rectitude maintained by that same snobbery, the settled conviction that one must, or at least should, accept restrictions to the temptations of the moment because of one's own superiority to most others. Egalitarian snobbery has, of course, ruled old-fashioned snobbery out of court. But everything has its price, so that egalitarian snobbery was bought with a rejection of civility.

What has also been ignored is the racial and ethnic group substitute for the exclusion inherent in class behavior. The following claim is not at all extravagant: the near disappearance of social class has created new forms of collective assertion. Rousseau's vision of acrimony dissolving in tears of brotherly reconciliation will not take solid form.

Maslow's Scale

Human beings remain creatures who are both self-centered and opportunistic. Depending upon how they perceive the strength of outer barriers (suppression), or the much less sharply realized inner ones (repression), they probe to see how far they can go. Suppression has always predominated over repression, despite the touching modern faith that suppression never has worked and never can work.

A. H. Maslow in his "A Theory of Motivation" in the *Psychological Review* (v. 50, 1943) stated five universal goals which he said deserve the name of basic "needs": physiological, safety, love, esteem, and finally self-actualization—or self-realization, arranged in a hierarchy of prepotency. Each need will, in sequence, monopolize consciousness and organize the capacities of the organism until it is gratified. When a "need is fairly well satisfied, the next prepotent (higher) need emerges in turn to dominate the conscious life and to serve as the center of organization of behavior, since gratified needs are not active motivators" (page 395).

Maslow warns that his schema is a statement about general tendency, and will throw little light on why any individual acts as he does. It will not, for example, explain why some people will deliberately choose martyrdom and thus sacrifice all physiological needs; Maslow suggests that such men may have had all such needs gratified in earlier life. All he insists upon is that "the person will *want* the more basic of the two needs when deprived in both."

It follows, for which Maslow is not responsible, that when the human being is told that he is suppressed from satisfying either esteem or self-realization (not needs at all but constant wishes), he will tend to transfer the urge to self-aggrandizement to some hostile and collective basis. If class striving is closed off, and striving within the division of labor is ideologically compromised, the drive to exclude as well as include will prompt many to seek out "my own people" in a heightened racial or ethnic-group identification. Such an emendation to Maslow's seminal contribution appears to be justified, at least by events.

2

SELF AND FAMILY

Ever since Cooley and the other symbolic interactionists there has been a way to avoid the futile heredity vs. environment controversy. Later studies of maturation have broken down the false dichotomy even further. The child's delayed humanity absolutely requires something more than either or both, and that is a lasting relationship with close adults. He is not born human, nor can he later find the gift of speech by himself. All he can utilize unaided are a few involuntary acts, such as crying and the Babinski reflex. Without protracted care and tutelage he would not even survive.

THE CHILD BECOMES HUMAN

The child is born an isolate. At first he does not distinguish among his own body, the crib, and the warm maternal presence. With the universal myth of omnipotence he at first believes that his own imperious wants produce the immediate ministering to his needs. The myth is never shattered, but it is broken when prohibitions are enforced by those around him whom the child subliminally begins to introject within his developing self. Shortly thereafter he learns the painful lesson of clashing interests; even a

The Nature of Morality

loving father may demand a quiet household when he is tired so he can get some rest.

However grudgingly, curbs must be accepted. When these gradually come to be self-prohibited actions and even thoughts, conscience begins to form, ultimately through identification with those persons who transmitted the prohibitions. Since the family gets the organism first, the family for the most part starts both self- and personality-development. Basic attitudes (although less certainly traits), loyalties, prejudices and point of view are here largely established. Later experience erects a superstructure upon a foundation.

Again, a paradox: the isolated self is not thereby erased and it cannot be. The developing self is never replicated in the image of those who first control it, and self-assertion later quickens. Others, then, will seek compliance from a self which is always tempted to withdraw (within limits imposed from outside itself), to assert its own individuality, to separate from George Mead's generalized other. The myth of central position, unlike that of omnipotence, is never broken.

The myth of central position is a continuous requirement for living with zest, for pursuing goals with intensive purpose. In the purely hypothetical case that everyone should become enough "realistic" to understand, emotionally as well as rationally, exactly what his life amounted to in terms of time and space, all effort would cease and Freud's death wish would prevail. Fortunately, no one has ever become totally adjusted.

The child is not at all realistic in the above sense. His concrete world may be restricted, but he entertains no doubt about his central position. What is, is what he knows. Darwin's children expressed mild surprise to learn that their friends' fathers did not "do their barnacles"

Self and Family

every day. Within a tiny world the child acquires a "culture" in the same restricted and concrete way.

Immediate others assign him roles he is supposed to play. In addition he assumes certain roles for himself, an action affected to an unknown extent by his fixed heredity. He does not so much create his own assumed roles as he makes choices among what is available, and normally resists one or more of the various roles assigned to him which are inconsistent with his choice. He may, for example, be expected by his mother to continue the role of nice, obedient little boy, which includes sitting on her lap, only to learn at school that other boys take a dim view of such compliance.

Finally, the child in imagination, fantasy, and play projects his role behavior into the future. He plays at the roles of the older persons whom he knows or has read or heard about. Despite all attempts in some circles to disparage such behavior, the little girl spends a lot of time playing mother with her dolls, while the little boy in imagination throws a touchdown pass as thousands shout themselves hoarse.

That is how the child completes the process of becoming a human being and acquires his private version of culture: from acting out with the others about him assigned and assumed roles, and from playing at adult roles. The child's world is concrete, specific, dramatic, and personal. Children at six or seven find it difficult to define even things, except for their immediate use, such as a chair being something to sit on. At eleven or twelve most children can define things and events logically, but only at approximately fourteen can a child define such an abstraction as patriotism.

This particular abstraction is ultimately based upon legends of his nation's glorious past, at one time more dependably taught is school than at a later time. Such indoctrination was enforced by identification with such concrete models as the wind-and-snow-torn Washington, brooding over the anguished faces and bloody tracks of his troops at Valley Forge. Or he became an American Marine while playing war games with his peers in an open lot. It was only because many concrete roles had become embedded in his self that as an adult he could thrill to a marching band and the unfurled standard whipping in the wind. Attachment to other abstractions is arrived at in a similar dramatization of self.

The Limits of Shared Humanity

Beyond what is universal in human nature, there are two structural factors which preclude common humanity from becoming the great uniting force. The first one is a cross-cultural appreciation for not taking the rules too seriously. Even house-broken people can achieve gratification by disclaiming whatever rules may be. Forbidden fruit tastes best; in Freud's acid phrase we are not forbidden to do what we do not want to do. Luther complained that the Devil has all the best tunes, and so it is that no man has ever boasted of being a Joseph. Ever since the prototype left his cloak in the outstretched grasp of Potiphar's wife, the "virtuous" male has been an object of ridicule. People who make a point of "being good" don't get along well at all with others. Mark Twain warned them that they would be lonely.

People remain ambiguous, to employ an overworked word, throughout their lives. During services the Protestant minister boasts about having been quite a fellow before he reversed his collar, or hints at the terribly dark

Self and Family

sins of his youth. His situation duplicates that of the Trobriand Islander who, when the boys get together, boasts about getting away with incest, defined by Trobriand sensibility as unspeakable, whether within far extended degrees of kinship or not.

That Trobriand Islander, like the Protestant minister, nevertheless tries hard to keep the support of those people among whom he has a reputation to maintain. So does the juvenile delinquent who tries to be "bad" and neither wants nor can be given any reputation which would reflect alien standards of respectability. Proclaimed rules throw only a dim light upon a universal personal problem, that of acceptance among the people known and important to ego.

This need for close human contact is as critical as it is universal. Cooley argued that introspectives could withstand such aspiration, especially in prison, because of their special ability to communicate imaginatively with absent others. Later research, though, has stressed the uniform consequences of deprivation in active sensory deprivation. Beyond that, the inclusion-exclusion rule also holds.

The second structural factor which precludes common humanity from becoming a uniting force is the fact that rules which are supposed to govern behavior come in three tiers, and they are inconsistent with one another. The first comprises abstract sentiments, such as The Land of Opportunity, Honesty is the Best Policy, and so on. Sentiments of this kind have been said to be critical for maintaining consensus, and perhaps so; they are nevertheless easily flouted.

The second tier comprise moral rules, such as those enshrined in the Ten Commandments. But whether honoring one's parents or justifying the moral rightness of abortion, here is where the strenuous efforts of intellec-

The Nature of Morality

tuals, of newspaper editors, of all would-be controllers of public opinion, are concentrated. Finally, the third tier includes the operating codes of specific organizations, and since the division of labor has supplanted social class as the arena for status striving, these subtle and shifting standards are as adamant as they are difficult to learn. Some aspects of them always violate rules at the other two levels, especially when the collective fate of the organization requires flexibility in bamboozling the general public.

Thus while in our country the self can be extended to comprehend all those (in collective terms) at a distance, empathy is bound to be restricted. Extension tends to be hedged, limited to those with whom one can identify. Only in relation to ourselves, as Hume pointed out in his Third Treatise, can lively concern be extended to others. There is no passion in human minds such as a love for all mankind. At least no group has ever been formed on the basis of common membership in the species. One could be so organized only if some non-human collectivity challenged or threatened the entire planet.

All species which bond are aggressive. Flocks of birds are not aggressive and they do not form close ties. Even Christianity needs an out-group to affirm itself against, to preserve an active awareness that others are not with us, at least not with us yet. If all the world's people should be converted to Christianity, or, rather, if all the people in the world became Christians, the organized Christian Church would wither.

Thus while a world-state is conceivable, it is not possible, even though the nation-state does not comprise the outer limit of extension, of in-group inclusion. Some ethnic, racial, and social-class groupings, for instance, maintain loyalties across the boundaries of many states. Social-class inclusion-exclusion was once so acceptable

Self and Family

that the Stuarts openly identified more with foreign monarchs than with their own English subjects. As late as World War I, social-class identification at the top contested to some small degree the overriding appeal of patriotism. In late 20th century, the revelation of a centripetal and totalistic racism in Japan was balanced by the centrifugal ethnic-group hatreds which played an essential part in the breakup of the Russian Empire.

Centrifugal impulses appear to be as inevitable as centripetal tendencies are essential. The latter are especially necessary to protect the undeveloped self within the small closed group which determines how the socialized human being will be trained, what the morality transmitted to him will be. In this connection the biological mother or a surrogate must be closely, immutably, bound to the child. The required expenditure of time, patience, loving care, can be provided by no other arrangement, least of all by the state. Only a few times in history, Plato being the notable exhorter, failed experimentation in the early Israeli kibbutz the notable example, has the state been charged with this critical function.

MARRIAGE

Women have not fared well at the hands of philosophers. Their contributions, even their economic contributions, have generally been either discredited or at best ignored. The term spinster, for example, was a 17th-century coinage which signified an unmarried woman who, as a textile spinner, was the key but unacknowledged figure in what was the cottage industry of that time.

Besides ignoring the contributions made by women, the philosophers have tended to stress a direct relationship between the state and an individual who was viewed as being endowed with equality, without intervening encumbrances such as marriage and family, classes and local communities. Although Locke and Jefferson, unlike Hobbes, were favorably disposed toward religion, at least that of a non-contentious sort, they failed, as did Hobbes and Roussseau, to describe the individual woman and man in marriage as the ultimate source of morality and thus of order.

That consideration aside, in history almost all women have been forced to prepare for the housewife-and-mother role, since nothing else was available. The spinster (later definition) was at best an object of pity, living out a lonely life with duty-bound relatives. The pressure to marry at any cost made for desperation, but more to the point there were uncounted thousands of women who married while secretly longing to work independently in the world. If the desire persisted, they made their husbands as miserable as themselves. In short, the option of single independence can be reckoned a blessing of the 20th-century's second half. Given the short span of allotted life, a stable social order is not necessarily in the interest of a given individual.

Militant feminists in late 20th century, on the other hand, stood on shaky ground to announce that all women feel depressed and unhappy when in "legal bondage to a man." Of course there is underlying discontent. But that is much less the result of women's traditional lot than it is a resentment of the human, the common condition, despite the concern expressed by those ancient Greek male dramatists who depicted a female loathing of patriarchy that was murderous.

The point is that in late 20th century there was no patriarchy. Those unfortunate men who were trained to expect "the little woman" to wait on them usually ran into serious trouble. The housewife-and-mother role had been almost universally displaced in the West by the partnership role, and men were expected, expected themselves, to help with whatever chores around the house needed to be done.

At the same time, the leadership of the feminist movement, made up of successful career women who either hated men or who claimed "You can have it all" (that is, career, marriage, and children), continued to stake the claim that they were the women who represented all women. They ignored differences of .temperament, occupational capability, and aspiration. Most married women, at some time or other, did work outside the home—in order to maintain a family income undermined by the tax policies of the state. They were not career women, in either ambition or result. They saw achievement elsewhere than in a paid job outside the home.

That particular social distinction among married women is an important one. Most women and men form a partnership to share a magic which soon transmutes into something more important; the raising of children. And if they are devoted to each other they can achieve a successful marriage, which can only be described elliptically, as did Andre Maurois in his reference to a long conversation that seems too short.

Sex

If there was one unavoidable subject in late 20th-century America, it was surely sex, very serious stuff indeed. Love was not so readily discussed. The late Willard Waller once remarked that anyone who discusses love in a serious way is bound to fall flat on the wrong side of the folk humor. On the other hand, solemn and humorless writer-engineers on the subject of "making love" are spared guffaws, no matter whether their detailed plans of position and posture, of counterposition and counterposture, appear about as relevant as a map of the tactics employed at Gettysburg. The fact is obvious, the reason why obscure.

Obscure too is the connection between sex and love, despite the determination shown in the popular arts to make them synonymous. Marriage does do an indifferent job of controlling the sex drive, which at one time was blamed only on men, who, torn between lust and love, are at least initially appalled at the thought of settling down and becoming a provider. The pursuit of happiness, according to Theodor Reik, means new women, and men are ever prepared to take on the next candidate. The dread of some feminists is amply justified: men are not to be trusted.

For thousands of years, until late 20th century, the assumption held that the male sex drive is more imperious and indiscriminate than that of the female. The earlier Kinsey studies stated so in a series of neat tables. With a relatively firm base in the family, that assumption (or myth, as the preponderance of written opinion held in late 20th century) served to keep down the number of illegitimate children brought into the family by wives. Wife as well as husband regarded her adultery as a much more disloyal act than his; the adulterous wife was thought to surrender to another man, the adulterous husband more likely to surrender to a temptation stripped of personalistic choice. The besetting sin of the male was thought to be lust, that of the female, vanity, in the form of "something better than the boy next door," or stark envy in the eyes of her sisters as she flaunted baubles showered upon her by some vague benefactor.

Self and Family

FEMINISM AND IDEALIZATION

While most women continued to settle for the boy next door and most men got married and stayed married, the feminist movement more or less successfully challenged an ages-old belief that female sexuality is less imperious than that of the male. Feminists denied anything but superficial and non-functional biological differences. Thus it was that feminism and the sexual revolution fed upon each other.

If sex differences are minimal or even lacking, why shouldn't women adopt the presumed male attitude toward sex? Dominated by patriarchy long enough, women should enjoy absolute equality in this as well as every other sphere. Women researchers showed that women were committing a larger percentage of all violent crimes than previously. It could be proved that women were just as dangerous as other people.

Not all feminists, of course, endorsed every cross-current to appear, most notably in the battle over equality vs. superiority. In very late 20th century Goddess worship surfaced, accompanied by the claim made by a minority of feminists that female figures in all conventional religions were almost absent. Identified male traits such as aggressiveness (Jesus of Nazareth?), were to be shunted aside in favor of identified female traits, such as nurturing, compassion, and intuition. Without realizing it, the more extreme ideological feminists were caught between an insistence that sex differences are so slight as to merit no attention, and an equal insistence that women are not only very different from men but superior to them.

An older dispensation emphasized superiority too, that is, moral superiority. In the fading myth of the old West, the West that never was, men engaged in armed combat and saloon girls while all other women represented family and church. There was never any doubt about which side, not always in the preference of the audience, would win.

Throughout the 19th century women were universally regarded as being morally superior to men. They were the leaders in all of the reform movements outside the home: anti-slavery, temperance, the organization of missionary societies and settlement houses, and the improvement of public education. Only when women's influence outside the home was dismissed as unimportant and irrelevant was the erstwhile strictly male province of work outside the home made an emotional lodestone to all women of even mildly feminist persuasion.

For centuries the proposition that women are morally superior held fast, doubtless for reasons of convenience as well as idealism. Women must embody superior moral rectitude, above all else in sexual matters. The legendary love affairs of literature always featured the inaccessible she. The Mother of God, in the Christian tradition, could only have been the Virgin Mother. Idealization, of whatever magnitude, presupposes some degree of continuous restraint.

Hypocrisy in this area, to be sure, has always achieved magnificent heights. Idealization of women, given the imperious sex drive, seems to rise and fall with hypocrisy. The Victorian idealization of women was accompanied by impressive rates of prostitution, pornography, and exploitation of women, sexual and economic, in domestic service. Shakespeare's period, in contrast, did acknowledge the accessible she, but note that Shakespeare avoided his own difficulty by describing Doll Tearsheet as a woman of a certain age and Juliet as a girl young enough to be a virgin.

Historically, promiscuity has been a function of social

Self and Family

class. Who bulls the cow must keep the calf may have been accepted folk wisdom of the 17th-century countryside, but it failed to control many males of the highest and the lowest orders. It has been established that a collectivity can support a promiscuous minority that is walled off by privilege or by the lack of any class status at all. What is not yet known is whether group survival can indefinitely accompany a self-righteous and nearly universal promiscuity.

One reason for the last claim is the adoption by militant feminists of dubious means to achieve the ends they proclaim. Insistence upon legal assignment of children to the divorced wife is a case in point. Men have less "instinct" to remain with their children than do women, and in their forties, unlike women, they are capable of starting a second family. The rule of male custody at one time controlled any impulse to avoid his established responsibility, and he was thus usually dissuaded from taking a younger woman.

Perhaps advisedly so. Many men, tempted to take a younger woman, have lived to regret that action. How can anyone relate to another person who hasn't been there and cannot share remembrance? What, in the words of one disillusioned husband, is there to talk about? There is also the crude matter of a sex-performance difference that can hardly improve with the passage of time.

In any event, feminists have weakened the father's tie to his children. Since he can more readily escape responsibility, he is more likely than once he was to seek divorce. Achievement of female custody is not so much a victory over patriarchal domination as it is a blow against protection for the wife. Feminists have subverted the male's bond with his children in another way. They say that abortion is no concern of the family, abortion being solely a female decision, in as well as outside of marriage. At the same time they lobby to keep all legal male responsibilities for that child if the wife's changing whim should be to bring it to term. The acrimony and hatred engendered by this one issue has become impressive.

A case for self-inflicted defeat can also be made about pornography. Feminists view it correctly as degrading to women, as an insulting expression of contempt. But feminists cannot afford to express too much revulsion, because the people who *are* engaged in a struggle against pornography are mostly outraged squares, people they would prefer not to be identified with. In this connection, as in so many others, feminists are caught in a dilemma. The people with whom they do ordinarily identify, free rebellious spirits who are individuated hedonists, include those who promote commercial pornography.

More than in any other aspiration, women, especially feminists, have been losers in the sexual revolution, even though the fear of getting pregnant is no longer the deterrent it once was, and they have been assured that sex can be made safe from disease as well. They are not often told, or choose to ignore because they have come to believe in the persecution of patriarchy, about universal appreciation for the unmarried woman's limited sexual experience. Preliterates and assumed preliterates, despite Margaret Mead's fabrications about free love in Samoa, take this matter quite seriously, and so do all civilized peoples.

It has been said that young American men no longer do, but they have developed a contempt for women—exemplified in so-called date rape—that has no precedent. If they all put out for anybody, why turn me down? It has not been demonstrated that feminism and sexual revolution is a workable combination. When most women at the outside work place were assumed to be unavailable, for ex-

Self and Family

ample, sexual harassment was not the serious condition it later became.

Why did so many non-working young women make themselves available to all comers? The most convincing argument was one that became ideologically indefensible. Young women throughout history have been disposed to please others, and they still are. While at one time they were praised for remaining virtuous, today they have been convinced that others will be pleased if they become a handy mattress.

As manners and morals steadily deteriorated, there was one change which only apparently reversed that trend. Why was the sexual conduct of all politicians more thoroughly searched than ever before, and more viciously denounced when any dirt could be uncovered? Such media treatment had nothing at all to do with traditional morality, but was fanned by a general feminist conviction that women have been treated lightly, have been used and abused, and no public figure should be permitted to get away with anything so abhorrent.

In late 20th century feminists made indignant demands for *legal* protection in order to go anywhere and behave as they pleased. Before they became openly available and with foul language one of the boys, they had that protection in the respect of most of the men they knew. When that respect was withdrawn, they got plenty of TV advice on how they might protect themselves from rape when they visited a man in his room. They were not advised to avoid visiting men in their rooms. All that could reasonably be asked, it was assumed in ideologically regnant circles, was that people be assisted in minimizing the risks associated with their own self-destructive behavior, say by the distribution of condoms at public expense to homosexuals, drug users, and young children.

The Nature of Morality

The feminists, like everyone else, would like to have the cure for their bellyache both ways. But for them the business of rape is crucial. One book has accused all men, from the beginning of time, of having systematically taught their sons to rape women. That charge raises another issue: Is the educated mind one that is open or closed? The writer of the book cited obviously wants to "raise consciousness" to the question of "male dominance" which, if consciousness is raised enough, becomes rape. Does an educated mind properly "engage in dialogue" with such a claim, or read a review of the book and dismiss it?

Feminists have better arguments than that. They are, for example, understandably resentful of even the vestigial double standard. But so long as a large proportion of women find, if nothing else, some economic advantage in getting married, the ancient male hope of pre-marital conduct in his wife that was superior to his own may be expected to continue.

As the perfume advertisement which had a big play in late 20th century insisted: "What makes a woman irresistible is the ability to admit she's wrong even when she knows she's right." This kind of thing drives feminists up the wall, but it also puts a cap on the women's movement. Now and for time to come a majority of women will gain more in the entire range of competition by such behavior than by equal competition with men—even though many of them are motivated to do it, are good at it, and relish the game at which they succeed. The ones who err are those who think all other women must be motivated in the same way.

The slight edge still held by so-called male dominance may be neither just nor fair. Admitted, too, that any vestige of the double standard is likewise neither just nor

Self and Family

fair. Ridiculed or denied, it has stayed. There are to be sure many very progressive young men who say they don't care about the past history of whatever woman they may some day marry. Presumably resigned to the inevitable, they are lying.

And they are confused. The freebooting male attitude toward sex may be ineradicable, but it can be tamed by a wife who is idealized for being potentially faithful. She is the only one who can offer a husband an overriding reason for remaining constant, because he would risk losing more than he could gain by doing what comes naturally. But with no conceivable basis for such idealization, why should any young man get married and stay married if he expects his wife to bring to their union what historically would have been a deserved reputation as a public convenience?

There is no way to determine what the immediate future of the feminist movement might be, because throughout history there have been many returns to ideologies which had been apparently superseded. All that can be said is that in late 20th century there seemed to be a gathering rejection of militant feminism, not, say, of equal pay for equal work but of equal pay for comparable work, accompanied by a rejection of gender hatred. Perhaps there was also a gathering suspicion of the militant minority's overwhelming power and influence.

In any event, the Census Bureau informed that two-thirds of married (not single) mothers worked only part-time or not at all. According to a confirming poll, a majority of all working women would prefer to remain at home. College girls were reported to be less responsive than before to the assumption that militant feminists represented all women. But again, any conceivable major shift to traditional roles would require a shift in perceived interests, and against a massive propaganda effort.

Dreams and the Electronic Media

How much the confusion of the young in late 20th century owed to movie and TV entertainment could not possibly be stated, much less measured. Defenders of the electronic media argued that they simply reflected changes in attitudes which had already occurred. The young, on the other hand, rather consistently ape the thought and gestures they see portrayed in the movies and on TV, now as in previous decades. In either event, during the 1930s and 1940s the central Hollywood myth of grand consummation always was marriage, and any previous hankypanky (only between the principals) was quite sedate and controlled by the girl. By late 20th century, young lovers depicted in a contemporary setting were, without exception, involved in a one-night stand or were shacked up.

Usually they practiced deceit and betrayal. The conventional denunciation of "all that sex and violence" missed a large point: these people did not trust each other, and they were not expected to. In some extreme cases they might "make love" while each planned to kill the other. Whatever then happened was supposed to be funny.

Idealization of some other must have been made difficult for the young, who were being systematically taught to rush at one another with mouths already opened for the exchange of oral fluids, and who were told to expect betrayal on all sides. Oddly enough, in those places whence the word-and-image flow emanated, the commercial attempt to undermine sensitivity and inhibition was proclaimed to be a liberation from Victorian suppression:

Self and Family

the writhing bodies of the electronic media represented courage and freedom.

The common people became particular victims of the feminism and sexual revolution combination. The wages of sin have never been exacted in a just fashion. People of wealth, either earned or unearned, have always had privileges denied to the common people, a condition that an era of aggressive egalitarianism failed to change appreciably. Daughters of the rich, and women feminist leaders, could afford to be liberated women because others hastened to clean up the messes they created. They did not have to pay the kind of price demanded from girls of ordinary background.

A mill-worker's daughter, for example, will likely pay a very high price for buying the feminist and sex-revolution combination. She has learned that she should rise above petty considerations of patriarchal marriage and outmoded morality. But her circumstances, including her own goals, such as treasured photos of a formal wedding (the most important day in her life), and the very unliberated men she knows, leave her with no resources of protection if she should rebel. Those writers of textbooks who prattle about the new promise of innovation, of homosexual marriage as well as trial marriage, officially-acknowledged group marriage, and about government-bureau responsibility for whatever children might unfortunately result from the new freedom, have known a restricted range of people.

We deal with dreams, wishes, visions, fantasies, even illusions, that is to say, with human beings. The inaccessible she was rarely all that inaccessible, a not altogether unfortunate circumstance. There never was a time when plastic-wrapped virginity was a gift to more than a few bridegrooms, and such a magnificent proof of non-arousal may not always have been much of a gift. Women, historically, have been prone to minimize or even deny their previous involvements which, according to those inevitable surveys (there are surveys for every taste), were never regretted if no price had to be paid for them. The secret self has its own reasons.

But the central issue never was the technical matter of tissue-involvement, only the possibility of idealization in married love. Anyone stupid enough to play the game of numbers would invite Waller's risk. At the same time there is a qualitative gap between, on the one hand, the girl who in the old-fashioned phrase has made a mistake, and on the other the girl who flaunts a record of many bodies in many different rooms. True enough, because of the vestigial double standard the woman may still be held to task more than the man, but every marriage starts out with two strikes against it when either party has been openly promiscuous. Impersonal sex is the worst school for marriage, that most personal of all relationships, the ultimate social compact.

LOVE AND TRUST

Love can be many things, appear in many guises. Love is not love that alters when it alteration finds, yes, but that is not the kind of love the world is seeking. And love, no matter how defined, is not nearly so rare as trust. Many of the 17th-century gentry who got bastards of country girls, for example, loved them in one way or another, but those girls could not trust the one whom they loved in return.

Neither love nor trust in getting people married was so dependable in the past as necessity. Santayana's laconic observation—that most men seem to avoid as long as possible the domestic bliss they crave—was a product of

Self and Family

the 20th century. Getting people married to stay married was much easier when they lived with outside pressures of closely-knit communities and social-class requirements, when production united two adults within the home instead of dispersing them, and when children were economic assets instead of being heavy liabilities.

In contrast, especially during the last quarter of the 20th century, marriage had to depend upon sentiment and a high order of felicity in order to achieve the craved domestic bliss. The lucky ones, those who made good marriages, had to discover who or what was finally responsible. The responsible ones were individuals, who could not depend upon a supportive network of institutions. They were supported by little more than trust in each other, an amazing phenomenon in a milieu where narcissism, and official sanctification of the lone self as arbiter and judge of all "values," became approved doctrine.

Despite, because of, the combined incitements of feminism and sexual revolution, the young by their own anguished admissions deeply distrusted one another to the same degree that they longed to trust someone, anyone. But how achieve trust when feminism scoffed at self-control, while it demanded that the state and its courts protect women no matter what they chose to do? How achieve trust while the sexual revolution promoted frequent change of partner? There was thus much floundering about, reflected in the trailer of a movie: "Two young girls, tired of casual sex, seek Mr. Right at a wealthy singles resort." Good luck.

There was a great hunger for the right one, the trustworthy one, which apparently grew as the means to reach her or him were spurned. And the handling of sex was only the beginning of their quandary. Most of the seekers of trust failed to realize (who would have told them?) that

The Nature of Morality

married trust is much more than sexual faithfulness. An assumed sexual fidelity only symbolizes an absolute and unquestioning mutual protection and support. Trust in marriage can thus only be created. It is not something to be discovered, not out there to be found. Mr. Right is not waiting at a wealthy singles resort.

Validated trust, in or out of marriage, is a rare thing even at the best of times, forever beyond the reach of any survey or poll. It is the rare person who finds more than one or two people in whom he knows he can place absolute trust. A discredited source provides the evidence. The Bible constantly enjoins us to love one another; the New Testament stresses this theme above all others. But there is not one word in this book of distilled folk wisdom about trusting one another. Trust can be placed only in the Lord.

With one another, very close others, bread cast upon the waters helps, but that old stuff became unacceptably old-fashioned. Meanwhile, there was love. Everyone sought it, some in desperation; some even demanded what only can be given, or they waited for someone, somewhere, perhaps the next one, to confer it.

But what is it? Cupid wears a thousand masks, manifold disguises for one endocrine system to call to another. When the expectation of trust is added, disappointment and even betrayal usually ensues. Until its mutual creation becomes unmistakable, trust itself can invite betrayal. Mutual trust rests upon a base of accepted restriction to any conceivable contrary impulse. It wears an open countenance that forsakes any mask. Since Americans in late 20th century lacked outer suppression of any consequence, repression in the name of mutual trust became a voluntary act. The greatest personal tragedy of late 20th century was no lack of love, but of trust.

The only analogue to marital trust is the experience of

combat soldiers. Published reminiscence always celebrates a time when a man had absolute trust in the man next to him, who could be depended upon without even being watched. Lost causes in this connection are especially cherished. No abstraction affects the matter, neither does the retrospective judgment of history. Nazi reports of time remembered differ not at all from those written by Americans. Remembered trust takes veterans of any cause back to old reunions and older cemeteries. Civilian life in contrast, with its on-the-make chicanery and manipulation, its hidden intentions and contrived sellouts, appears contemptibly shabby.

Happy Marriage

The evidence about what makes a good marriage has been available for some time. Not lack of evidence, but reluctance to face it, especially among the well-educated, has led to a general ignoring of the evidence. The ancient news was announced back in the 1930s, when Burgess and Cottrell (*Predicting Success or Failure in Marriage*) and Lewis Terman and his associates (*Psychological Factors in Marital Happiness*) reached conclusions identical with those published in obscure places during the 1990s. By unwitting convergence, both of the earlier books characterized "happy" husbands and wives as almost perfectly fitting the Victorian ideal of proper conduct.

"Happy" husbands are stable, do not gamble but save their money, are methodical rather than impulsive, and are willing to assume responsibility. They remain traditional in their attitudes toward sexual, moral, and religious matters. "Happy" wives are kindly, cooperative, church-going, and not given to rivalry and domination. They are methodical, painstaking, and traditional in their attitudes toward sexual, moral, and religious matters. A dull bunch perhaps, but they got what they paid for.

In this regard the times have not changed at all. Only people educated far beyond their capacity to learn can ignore the obvious, the glaring, connection between a traditional outlook and successful and happy marriage. Marriage, and its accompanying family, are the most conventional arrangements that people have developed over the centuries. These arrangements are not, never were and never will be, a haven for malcontents.

3

RELATIVISM AND THE FAMILY INSTITUTION

Relativism has become the dominant intellectual approach to reality. Modern people, even traditionalists, have been taught to look for underlying causes, to find reality beyond proclaimed facts. Behind every surface explanation lies the true explanation, if anyone's truth can be trusted. Ultimately, any truth may be created at will, so long as it departs widely enough from received wisdom.

RELATIVISM

At the very least those who are young enough to be educated in the modern world do not look far outside of themselves to discover truth. In a famous revolutionary statement Marx said we must create truth instead of trying to find it. A version of the same idea appears in the now ubiquitous term "values." Values are not supposed to be necessarily true, nor even shared. They merely indicate preference, usually personal preference. Values become such when anyone announces them as such. Note that the common coin used establishes nothing beyond personal preference.

Neither values as preference, nor relativism more broadly conceived, need be the nihilistic trap that is often assumed. Even that standard ploy of Philosophy 101, pointing out the independence of value from fact, carries no moral imperative whatsoever. When polar bears are disappearing some people will hasten to protect the species, while others will go out to shoot one before it is too late, in order to adorn an empty wall with a trophy. If all is relative, and values are nothing but personal preference, then "environmentalism" has only a debatable moral basis.

In his piece "A Free Man's Worship" Bertrand Russell himself violated the rules of Philosophy 101 when he begged people to treat one another in a kindly fashion *because* there is no other source of caring in the universe. But in anticipated rebuttal, Dostoevski said that if God is dead then anything is permitted. The conditional is appropriate.

That there must be some kind of moral imperative in relativism is an erroneous assumption. The *fact* that distant others may live by standards which differ from our own, for example, does not necessarily mean that their standards are superior, or that their standards should be praised and followed. Possibly those distant others simply made some bad choices. Why, as the Mead-Benedict followers have it, should we live more like simpler peoples, or Third World countries? Why shouldn't they live more like us? In either case, we deal solely with prejudice. It is essential that relativism be relativized, with relativistic arguments turned around.

Admitted, the drift of modern education makes high waves. The "clarification of values" denies all validity to even shared preference. Everyone becomes his own legitimate judge of what seems right for him. But again, the moral imperative is lacking. The famous talk-show host—who interviewed lesbian nuns and then aggressively insisted that they are good Catholics, their practices being unfairly proscribed by a misguided Church establishment—failed to provide one.

The *fact* that there are lesbian nuns confers no license to select among what rules to believe and which to obey, no right to be accepted on one's own unconditional terms by an institution built upon dogma but which has always welcomed the acknowledged and penitent sinner. If each "clarifies his own values," and what he represents to himself is morally right to him, then the next person is not required to accept or even to accommodate to those values because his own values must—ours is, after all, a democratic society—be equally sacrosanct. Out of total chaos then comes order: everyone is free to condemn what he perceives as wrongdoing.

The most important theme of relativism has meanwhile gone unexamined: control of what will next happen varies with the number of players involved. The more people, the less control by any one person. In the big picture of massive social change, intrusions from outside occur regardless of anyone's wish or preference. New coalitions of perceived interests and opportunities to gain power then emerge. Because people are subject to a multitude of contradictory impulses they can turn their unsettled world upside down.

The total collapse of Soviet economy in 1989 precipitated such a massive change of perception. For almost fifty years the Western imagination had been gripped by a certainty of cataclysm resulting from a power confrontation between America and the Soviet Union. The big picture, at the later time, demanded a reorientation of attention, in some quarters inconveniently. Calculations had to be redrawn, and the world had to be viewed in a new way.

The Nature of Morality

Similarly massive events occurred in late 17th and late 18th centuries. What had almost universally been agreed in 17th-century England—that open discussion of the variant religious loyalties could not be accommodated—amidst emotional exhaustion suddenly became possible. Late 18th-century France was even more problematical. Hysterical bloodletting in the cause of insatiable abstractions was followed by national unity and a military discipline that transformed Europe. Human nature is so volatile, as well as being contradictory, that other seismic shifts of collective attention await the next conjuncture of intrusion, perception of new reality, and newly perceived interest.

Control over what will happen next varies with the number of players. Even an ultimate wielder of power can be more pushed by all those contesting others than he directs them. Small groups, especially members of a family, are exempted from at least that kind of insecurity. Ends and their means are, always speaking relatively, surely guided. Such lurching surprises as unanticipated and unwanted results seldom occur.

An ability to make a difference is one of the great attractions of the family. No matter if they are temporarily under siege, some will always seek domestic felicity. No matter how successful their declared adversaries may have been, especially in turning over traditional family controls to the state, there always will be those who share the perspective of C. S. Lewis. He found the very justification of life in the overlooked corners of the big picture. Lewis never denied the big picture, nor the need to participate within it. At the same time he judged it by how often in brief ages of confidence those celebrations of the small scale were permitted to appear in the corners.

In his written work the big picture's big problems, with

every solution dragging along a train of new ones, go ignored. He knew that big problems are never solved, that the conditions of permanent dilemmas are only rearranged. This eloquent defender of the concrete and the particular avoided any scheme to save the world on its own terms. He lived apart from any vision of a collective tomorrow supposed to fulfill one or another abstraction; he lived with here and now, and certainty of an eternity which Einstein and Bertrand Russell admitted they could not disprove. His justification for civilization was tobacco and beer and local concerns shared with companions in a dingy pub, where mutual trust discloses the basis of all visible good.

Lewis was also a good family man. He provides one answer to that smart-aleck question: Why bring children into a world like this? So that they may enjoy life in their turn, and perhaps find what they will look for. Those who would break the chain of generations are the ones who entice disaster. To claim otherwise would be an egregious example of the psychologist's error, the belief that one's own interpretation of life must be shared by all others.

MARGARET MEAD (1901–1978)

Relativism in its social, popular, form received a compelling impetus from the work of Margaret Mead. True enough, the intellectual climate was eagerly receptive. But at the same time her own contribution to the dominance of relativism cannot be discounted. To an incalculable degree, what happened and when it happened must be attributed to her.

In 1975 anthropologist Eleanor Gerber, after fifteen months of field work in American Samoa, reported that her informants behaved in remarkably different ways from those described in Mead's *Coming of Age in Samoa* (1928). They told Gerber that impulsive actions had been even more punitively restricted back in the twenties. This highly-trained investigator rejected what she saw and heard, and concluded that for some inexplicable reason Samoan life must have totally changed. Her dilemma is stated in Derek Freeman's book, *Margaret Mead and Samoa* (Harvard, 1983), which has been much utilized here.

Utopia is not so old a source of human longing as Arcadia. Thomas Hobbes had argued the dominance of time past in the human imagination. No man can create a future, because it is not yet; only out of our perceptions of the past can we create a future. But that past can be as visionary as any perceived future utopia, as filled with illusions and idyllic promises. Arcadia, usually more political than Mead's essentially sexual construction of a primitive happy state, is affiliated with other myths, such as that of the Noble Savage, the Golden Age, the Fall of Man. In various ways these all speak of time lost when inequality and suffering did not exist, and of a hope that the past may be restored.

Although Arcadia is most often located in the past, Mead's variant of it is located in a timeless present. In this rescue from career there are no schedules, no imposed habits, no point in striving to make a scratch on the earth's surface when stretched out on warm sand. As the echo of distant screaming egos vanishes from memory, the tensions and restraints of civilized life easily fall away. Since contesting wills are banished, lots of sex can be enjoyed without obligation and therefore without guilt.

Mead's particular variant of the Arcadian myth is the place where an imagined paganism brushes against pornography, the most private part of the secret self. Freud

Relativism and the Family Institution

had already bought this vision, but Mead filled it in with bright colors. She did this almost solely in Chapters II, XIV, and especially in Chapter XIII ("Our Educational Problems in the Light of Samoan Contrasts"), by far the longest. In the internal part of the book, where her observations are recorded, she proved to be too good an ethnographer to permit her conclusions to interfere with them.

Of the twenty-five girls past puberty whom she regularly interviewed on the front lawn of the United States Naval Government pharmacist's house, where she rented a room, fourteen of them, she states, were virgins. Mead also tells about a cult of virginity celebrated around *taupos*, daughters of chiefs. All Samoans are members of the same Protestant sect, girls are chaperoned, and every phase of social life is "treated with punctilio." Mead also mentions a competition for honor, a rigid hierarchy of place and authority, and the punishments visited upon those who flout it.

Mead offers abundant evidence of puritanical attitudes toward sex, of jealousy, envy, suppression, rebellion and punishment, in short of a lot of storm and stress during adolescence. Such a picture, though, is drawn mainly when individuals are being described. Such observations are denied or softened to invisibility in her conclusions, which circumstance arouses suspicion that her mission was at variance with her evidence. Those modern Samoans who now attend college on the mainland have reacted with contemptuous hilarity to the Chapter XIII claims that Samoans favor casual, easily transferred emotional ties and that an "acceptance of promiscuity" is their way of life.

Freeman mounted his case with meticulous care. He used official Samoan statistics, carried back to the 19th century, on murder, rape, and assault. These rates have always been impressively high, despite Mead's claim that

The Nature of Morality

Samoans "lack deep feeling." Freeman viewed himself as faced by a tragedy he had to unfold. At one time he approached Mead with his preliminary findings and offered her an opportunity to refute them. She declined the invitation, and since the publication of his book no one has come forward to quarrel with his total dismissal of her theme on other than ideological grounds, as when the American Anthropological Society in national assembly *voted* against his book.

After *Coming of Age* there were more startling disclosures to come, which remain outside of Freeman's purview. In assessing sex roles among the Tchambuli of New Guinea, Mead said that in contrast to the usually expected pattern Tchambuli women are dominant and the men subservient to their wishes. On the other hand, the men are described in her *Sex and Temperament* (Morrow, 1935) as conducting intertribal trade, as recently having been headhunters before this amiable hobby was prohibited by the British, as constantly being on the verge of fighting among themselves and, since he is stronger, "a man can beat his wife . . ." (page 264). Their "patriarchal forms," which she admits are there, nevertheless remain "unreal."

The Tchambuli male who treats his women with ceremonial deference, who primps and preens and spends a lot of time on his hairdo, could be a soul brother of the Restoration dandy who, also, treated his women with ceremonial deference, and with lace-covered wrists arranged his long curly locks as he made ready to fight a duel. Mead apparently ignored the anthropological rule that a physical act or exhibited trait derives its significance from a total context of behavior and is not to be understood in isolation. But such nit-picking is beside the point. Book by book Mead more engaged politics than anthropology. In the Introduction to *From the South Seas* (Morrow, 1939) she announced: "The battle which we once had to fight with the whole battery at our command, with the most fantastic and startling examples that we could muster, is now won" (pages x-xi).

In the train of World War I's intrusion, Mead's own battle started with *Coming of Age*. During the twenties the intellectual-political stakes rose above what they had recently been. The utopian promise of Russia was featured in all but the crustiest magazines, while intellectuals in large numbers found the future there to be working splendidly. This was the time of the lost generation and the blue light at the end of the pier, of John Held cartoons, necking, bathtub gin, the Charleston and Frank Harris warning the flappers that if skirts got any shorter they would have two more cheeks to powder. But in retrospect this was still another time of innocence, mostly excited talk.

Despite the fake-pagan motif, Mead never attacked the detailed substance of American life in a frontal way. That task was forcefully taken up by such iconoclasts as Sinclair Lewis and Henry Mencken. They inveighed against provincialism, the wasteland of small-town Protestant America, whose stultifying religion they ridiculed. Booze was daring, sex even more so, and science, especially Freud, would save us.

The pictures then informing the minds of iconoclasts were not yet sick and despairing. Theirs was an exuberance in giggling at philistine boosters. They never promoted Marxism, only poked fun at those who were alarmed by it. The power of a new elite may have been emerging, but as yet it was constrained by their representing an educated minority among the benighted unlettered.

In the meantime Margaret Mead had studied for three years under Franz Boas, a true child of Enlightenment. In his 1883 field notebook he wrote of the Eskimo he was studying that it was "a difficult struggle for every individual and every people to give up tradition and follow the path of truth." He became the declared enemy of all biological explanations of human behavior, and Boas had lots of company. Trenches were being dug in the nature-nurture battle, while stimulus-response in psychology steadily pushed back instinctivism. Even though hereditarians, respectable ones as well as eugenicists, still vied for attention, a consensus was forming around the notion that malleable human nature could be directed into such rational channels as might be desired.

By the mid-twenties Boas's graduate students as professors reigned American anthropology with their ideology of absolute cultural determinism. Still, much remained to be done. On the faculty with him at Columbia, for example, Professor Franklin H. Giddings of the sociology department was promoting biological views of Anglo-Saxon preeminence and inveighing against further immigration; a former graduate student of Giddings in 1926 even published a book entitled *The Racial Basis of Civilization*.

One of the issues which bemused Boas was the connection between biological puberty and social behavior. Was a widespread assumption of inevitable storm and stress at puberty mistaken? Perhaps differences in culture, not universal physical development, could decide the answer. He wrote a letter in the summer of 1925 as Mead was preparing to sail, asking her to investigate that very matter. Mead nailed down the critical proof that biology could be dismissed; she demonstrated that adolescence in the United States was needlessly tragic as well as being socially malforming.

Mead's book crowned the triumph of cultural determinism. Or was that the real purpose of the coronation? There was, there remains, a hunger for the message that what you want to do is wrongfully forbidden. For over sixty years her book has renewed a shock of discovery, fulfilled Ludwig Lewisohn's definition of a classic as a book "whose vision the youth of successive generations can make its own." *Coming of Age* took in even middle-aged skeptic H. L. Mencken, who used Mead as a club to thump the Bible-thumpers.

Her enormous success, as well as that of Ruth Benedict, stems in part from the fact that, unlike most anthropologists, they were not studying, say, the Samoans or the Zuñi at all, but preaching to their own United States. These two close friends, fellow Boas graduate students, reversed the journey of the 19th-century missionary who brought the light of Western civilization to dark places. They instead picked out primitives, or at least "simpler peoples," whose contrasting ways taught us a great deal about what was wrong at home, about aggression (too much) and sex (not enough).

But was Mead justified when she announced in 1939 that "we" had won the battle? Not quite, for in one sense excited receptivity had won. And of course no intellectual victory ever goes indefinitely unchallenged. Nothing is ever settled once and for all. There are only fashions which appear or recur with political-ideological shifts in the struggle to define the moral basis of social life.

Still, the self-congratulation Mead indulged is understandable for her personal influence became truly awesome. That was why she could assume her "we" to have universal application, so that if ". . . we hold before us, as a goal, a world in which each gift will have its place, we may be able to make the necessary social inventions to construct a world of interrelated and integrated values

The Nature of Morality

which will replace both the homogeneity of the savage and the confused and frustrating heterogeneity of the twentieth century" (last Mead reference, pages xxx-xxxi). Here is the fully-expressed heart of Meadism. The whole world is a seminar room wherein Boas's conviction that truth shall conquer error through rational demonstration is brought to pass—although with their faith in the power of rational persuasion these people were closer to refuting themselves than they would have cared to admit.

Fortunately, particular cultural "forms may be given new direction by the human will . . ." A choice is available "for all those who think and care . . . for even remote generations of men" (page xxiv). For twenty years before the Restoration in England literally thousands of people vainly tried to make choices for remote generations of men. Skepticism is justified, if for no other reason than that Mead's syllogism falls apart: cultural determinism rules; each people is a product of a particular culture; so by rational function "we" can readily change what "we" do not like.

The script may seem absurd but it does have one shining virtue. Like everyone else MM (as she was known among the awed staff at the American Museum of Natural History) was of course primarily concerned about self, but there was little power urge in her unfolding public design. Mead had no fixed agenda. Like Eleanor Roosevelt and the later Aldous Huxley, she wanted people to improve themselves and their world in one way or another.

At no time did she lapse into utopian socialism. Hers was no hate-America crusade of the kind that would later enlist college students. Indeed she scolded "savages" as well as her fellow citizens when they behaved in ways she thought improper. Her advice shifted with ideological fashion: anti-Protestant restraint, generation gap, peace movement, and feminism in low key. During World War II she devised menus for the Clean-Your-Plate Club at the regional office of the Food Distribution Administration, which was located on Wall Street.

THE FAMILY AS INSTITUTION

A case could be made that nothing essential has changed since the 17th century, when most Puritan husbands loved their wives and had due regard for them. Their Puritan wives ran their own households, and were spared the tedium of always asking for more money. The unity of the family was highly prized. Extant diaries and biographies attest to shared purpose. In a tribute to his deceased wife Milton said: "But O as to embrace me she inclined/ I waked, she fled, and day brought back my night." A like social type, even in Paris throughout the Terror, kept faith with family and God.

However shared the traditional outlook may be across the centuries, the family as institution later fell upon hard times. Family breakdown in late 20th century became a most popular topic. The family invariably came first in a circle of finger pointing. Schools failed because the family had failed, or the breakdown of law and order was caused by a breakdown in the family, or the drug traffic enlisted new recruits because the family had lost control of its younger members.

Although America was less "racist" than any African or Asian nation, racism was said to be caused by stereotypes maintained within the American family. The family was a hot-bed of prejudice and needed to be curbed, for the family perpetuated gender and homophobic stereotypes as well. The importance of the family was admitted. What was missing was much of any acknowledgement of its central and total indispensability, with or without warts.

Other institutions, especially the school, had been charged for decades to take the lead in bringing about desired personal change. A famous commentator toward the end of the century wrote a piece advising changes in the public schools to ensure neatness, courtesy, self-discipline, and goal-oriented behavior for the slobs (his reasonable term) then to be found there in abundance. He did advise a family contribution to the running of public schools, of a kind which would be welcomed by very few public-school administrators.

More than two decades before the cited piece appeared, Harry Golden harked back to his own experience as a youth on the Lower East Side. He predicted that young blacks and Hispanics, given all the advantages of Great-Society legislation, would eagerly seize the opportunities offered by public libraries and the public-school system, as did the young Jews of his boyhood memory. Mr. Golden overlooked the unity and strength of the Jewish family, and its reverence for learning.

Harry Golden should not be faulted in his failure to imagine the unimaginable, that the public-school system would one day seek to undermine the family and even learning itself. According to an investigation funded by the United States Department of Education made in 1985, in all of the social studies texts adopted by California and Texas (the bellwether public education states), no reference was made to marriage as the basis of family life, so that such words as husband and wife, as housewife and homemaker, were not to be found. Career women and famous blacks were featured instead, as well as minority rights, feminism, and the physical environment. Radical femi-

Relativism and the Family Institution

nism by a long chalk was the main theme, and role reversal the chief topic of illustrations.

There was no celebration of Golden's entrepreneurship. No one worked hard except for self-enjoyment alone, with no voluntary charity ever expressed. Totally absent were rags to riches, successful immigrant boys, the ubiquitous Carnegie libraries, and Silicon Valley. These textbooks were politically correct, dumbed down, quite inaccurate, and sloppily edited. Public education was such that it made little difference.

The illusion that magic can be wrought by state expansion into all erstwhile family responsibilities has not faded with the passage of recent time. But the family is not one institution among others, any of which could readily substitute for it in the raising of children. The family instead is the bedrock upon which everything else rests; when civilizations crumble, they return to that base. How a man and woman united in responsibility for their own children choose to comport themselves is a measure of, a testing ground for, all subsidiary institutions. Doing the right thing within those small units became difficult in late 20th century, yet doing the right thing became even more essential within a collectivity which officially measured its worth on how much it deferred to those who would further weaken the family bond, and deferred as well to incompetents, losers, and malcontents.

Until the middle of the 20th century, marriage was much more status than contract, never revocable by mutual consent, affirming standards and obligations—especially to children born of the union—that bound together what Durkheim called the *conscience collective*. Then marriage became a contract between two people which could be terminated at will with so-called no-fault divorce. But small children were not covered by this contract, so they had to pay an involuntary price for the new freedom when their parents were encouraged to break their private contract with each other at their own convenience.

That encouragement occurred without popular demand. The revolutionary legal principle of no-fault divorce was independently developed by a coterie of lawyers and therapists, promoting private sets of agendas, who pushed it. Only later was that device adopted by radical feminists as a shibboleth for liberation, despite an undermining of the husband's responsibility for his own children and making of his seeking divorce an attractive option. Wives thus made free often became legally responsible for helping to liquidate pre-divorce debt. Under no-fault divorce the state still requires an exchange of vows as well as a contract, and then ignores both.

Small children cannot make a contract, are denied even a choice when their protection is withdrawn. The trust they have had in their parents is suddenly violated, and the critical problem of who must keep the first promise is raised in a cruel way. The child feels betrayed, and he is betrayed. He will soon perceive his future as being unprotected from his own and others' Hobbesian human nature.

An historic biological interdependence is destroyed. In particular cases, though, biological interdependence has proved to be more nominally than literally required. The determination of many childless couples to adopt children, and the mutual loyalty and trust which can develop from such adoption, indicate that any attempt to locate "shared genes" as the compeller of family solidarity is seriously flawed. Professor Edward O. Wilson, for one, has mathematically determined that family solidarity results by one half in the case of each biological parent, one fourth in the case of each grandparent, and so on.

What really unites any family, unless deterred by agents

from the outside world (there are forty couples anxious to adopt for every adoption permitted), is a fusion of personalities, whatever the biological relationship of the members may be. There are, unfortunately, biological parents who treat their children as garbage to be thrown away. It is thus the couple who are motivated to socialize the child who become his parents through continuous association, who determine most of what version of "culture" the child will acquire. Such an association is ordinarily best, but not necessarily, maintained through biological relationship. When other institutions discourage moral behavior, it is up to the family, whether biological or adoptive, to provide the needed guidance.

FAMILY REWARDS

Why should they? After all, we only go around once and everyone has a right to live his own life, right? Only very determined people could stare down such a challenge. They got no help from the "culture" nor the media, in most cases none from their own churches. They had to find their own way by retreating with others of like mind and tuning out all the progressive nostrums.

Decent Children

The rewarding joy of raising decent children was proved attainable by those parents who organized and ran private Christian schools. Their accomplishment was, however, widely misunderstood as well as misinterpreted. Books on the Christian-school development were invariably written by horrified detractors, by naive partisans, or by social scientists who chose to reduce the movement to nullity with professional jargon.

The Nature of Morality

The people who organized such schools often did so without leadership, help, or understanding from their own church authorities. Clergymen in late 20th century, understandably, were not often seeking leadership in traditional causes. They were more than likely to have made an accommodation to what Pitirim Alexandrovich Sorokin once called "the super-rotten phase of sensate culture."

The prevailing mood of outraged parents has been badly explained. It was defensive, not an intended threat to impose anything upon outsiders, only a determination to prevent those outsiders from harming their children. They did not want to enforce church upon state, only to resist the electronic media and the state from dictating what their children should believe. Their basic impulse was to be let alone within their own communities; not to force school prayers upon other communities, but to have prayers said in their own schools. If sodomy was blessed in San Francisco, they were not stirred to interfere with San Francisco, only to prevent San Francisco from exerting its political will upon their own local community. But their real, mostly unacknowledged, adversary was the battering-ram of egalitarian leveling, which was always used to smash any attempt to settle a controversial social issue within the local community.

The goal of raising decent children was agreed upon. The argument among themselves was about how to achieve it. In this particular, the plight of the school organizers resembled that of various 17th-century religious movements, whose leaders likewise could not overcome the indifference of those sympathizers they sought to proselytize. The old problem remained the same: other people would not see the light in the same way.

Some of these people, for example, opposed their fellows by promoting the use of politics to coerce others with the power of the state. A minority of this minority used political coercion to shut down abortuaries. But the urge to do good, when accompanied by the ancillary urge to control other people with the power of the state, not only led to moral compromise, especially in the case of abortion, but also to being sold out by politicians who wanted their votes but no part of fixed principle in what was, for themselves, a no-win situation. Actually, attempts to control distant others with political threat never became a high priority with Christian-school families.

They did their best when they shared a single objective and controlled the means applied to it, as in the case of their own schools. So far as the big picture went, they were neither sophisticated nor intransigent enough to threaten the political leaders they prayed God to guide. Their situation nevertheless resembled to some extent that of the Rev. Martin Luther King, Jr., who declared during a 1961 television interview that if the Supreme Court should ever declare the sit-ins to be illegal, that he would "appeal to the higher court of conscience."

Spoken like a 17th-century Puritan. It was in a smaller way that Christian-school parents had the potential to defy legal authority. In the unlikely event that any of their 15-year-old daughters had ever been caught hitchhiking on the open road, action to stop the practice would have been as unequivocal as the determination shown by the Rev. King. In their case, the latest misinterpretation of the Constitution by the Supreme Court of the United States, expanding the rights of minor children, would have gone ignored. They, too, would have appealed to the higher law of conscience.

To do what they did best, many of these people had to pick themselves up from the degradation of the Youth Revolt, by returning to the religious and moral training of their childhood, the only source of adult morality. Admitted: training a child in the way he should go does not work in every case. Sooner or later, however, in most cases that training works.

The people under discussion invested a lot of themselves in keeping as many youngsters as they could straight. They learned that it was still possible to raise children who are neat, respectful, free of drugs, goal-oriented, mischievous, and with intellectual curiosity unblighted. These children had full experience of the world delayed for them, so that they would not be overwhelmed by it. Their mentors proved that a boy can be taught to be respectful toward women who neither want nor deserve such attention, that a girl can be taught to know the predator from the good man, who as a husband will take care of her, as she will take care of him.

The parents of these children were not wealthy. They were common people who could not afford to pay taxes for public schools and at the same time pay even the modest cost of tuition at their own schools, where dedicated teachers (sorry: no other term will do) made half as much money as they could have made in the public-school system. Parents helped those teachers with money gifts and in the same way helped one another. Parents and teachers worked closely together, indeed much of the teaching was done by the parents themselves, on an unpaid part-time basis. Within their own limits they were testing that impossible paradox, of losing their own lives in order to gain them.

Those who controlled the word flow had no word for these people. The teachers were not interviewed, not even on any national TV Christian program. In Canada and the United States they were educating about 2.5 million children, whose academic performance on standardized tests

Relativism and the Family Institution

far outranked that of public-school attenders. These teachers made an economic sacrifice to do the job, and they never went on strike for higher pay. They, and the parents of the children they taught, were the forgotten men and women of their time.

Christian parents remained so desperate that where the state permitted teaching one's own children at home, many of them did so. In late 20th century a few politicians mildly stirred after testing the wind. Punitive taxation of families was in some quarters deplored. A few politicians cautiously questioned the wisdom of providing condoms in the public schools without parental knowledge or consent. More politicians than in the recent past put in a good word for "family values," and even questioned whether the state should continue to make production of multiple babies on welfare a profitable enterprise.

There was a countervailing outpour of rhetoric. Why punish the children? Why encourage abortion? The difficulty here was that prevailing progressive opinion did encourage abortion, especially when expressed by family-counselling practitioners. Many of them were clergymen who had lost their vocation and sought to do good in a secular enterprise. They rarely encouraged divorce, abortion, or the legal right of children to "divorce" their parents.

Most practitioners, however, were not clergymen. Like most college professors they were imbued with the attitudes of the rebellious sixties which had formed them. With few exceptions they were themselves divorced, and in either event they were proponents of radical individuation for everyone. They really believed that if everyone did his own thing that the world would be better off. Therapeutic advice from such people, for the most part hidden from view, served to counteract the pressures which could move the more visible politicians.

Escape from Social Pathologies

Should the extent of various social pathologies be interpreted with a statistical or moral yardstick? Illegitimacy seemed headed for statistical normality when in a thirty-year period it rose five times, so that almost one in four babies was born outside the family, when two of every three black children were thus prepared for life. Such children in their turn were much more likely to perpetuate illegitimacy, or to seek divorce if they did marry. Amidst the confusion, traditionalists always appealed to the moral definition (it's wrong), while progressives invariably endorsed the statistical (everyone's doing it), in order to justify their separate positions.

Meanwhile the evidence piled up that statistical measures of everyone's doing it, whether self-serving or models of verisimilitude, left begging the question of what the various social pathologies were actually doing to youngsters, and equally important, what the causal nexus of those pathologies might be. The uncoordinated evidence adduced by social scientists, in some cases with arched eyebrows of disbelief, was that the best protection for youngsters from AIDS, alcoholism, pre-marital pregnancy, becoming "homeless," from suicide and crime, was to be raised within a traditional family. A magnificent triumph of tautology was displayed in those correlations.

Children of divorced parents were found to be several times overrepresented in penal institutions. The children of mothers who remained in the home achieved markedly higher grades in school. Working-mother professionals were much less prone to have "sexually-active" teenagers if they held traditionally feminine jobs, such as nurses, secretaries, and school teachers. And child abuse was found to be almost incalculably more prevalent in "single-parent homes" than in those where both parents were in residence.

Studies and statistics—if any were needed—showed an intimate relationship between drug use on one hand, and divorce and illegitimacy on the other, in or out of the "inner city." And cohabitation before marriage, despite a drumfire of affirmative claims, failed to produce better marriages than traditional ones. Studies demonstrated that couples who lived together before marriage were by a long chalk more prone to divorce than their more respectable peers.

Some of the common people, anyway, required no further formal education to figure out what was going on. It was the reaction to the pathologies infesting their streets, not to reports appearing in arcane journals, that drove parents to found the Christian-school alternative to the public schools. These people did not want school clinics providing their children with contraceptives and abortion referrals without their being notified. They did not want those special school lectures where their children would be told that homosexuality reduces the danger of overpopulation. They were not prepared to be even rational about the possibility that someone might introduce their child to drugs. And they were tired of being told that as teenage pregnancy and venereal disease continued to climb in conjunction with more and more public-school training in how to avoid both, that they ("the family") were the ones responsible.

They were also turned off by the movies and TV. Most others apparently were not. The evidence about marital

The Nature of Morality

happiness and emotional stability, the child's need for the traditional home, most others largely ignored because it was repugnant to the ascendant sensibility, demonstrated by the predominant themes of the movies and television. Those themes depicted human beings talking, planning, and striving. The electronic media thus engaged instruction as well as entertainment, whether what they were doing was disclaimed or not. Either screen held up models of character and transmitted standards of conduct. Such instruction built habits of expectation and response, determined what the audience wanted as much as what the audience wanted determined the entertainment with which they were supplied. Some people, possibly a majority of them, can be led to want what they can get.

The basic message of the electronic media was this: Happiness and fulfillment should be sought by dropping everyone and everything else to chase the next momentary impulse. Ignore whatever risk may be of personal disaster, including venereal disease and the certainty of betraying others. Only a candle burning at both ends can give a lovely light, and jumping around rapidly can substitute for thought. Conversely, an orderly life disguises sinister or at best ridiculous motives, particularly when the murderer or child molester, or the poltroon, has been identified as a Christian or some other kind of square.

The electronic media were not alone in making mischief. Government and the courts, in effect if not intention, besmirched the traditional family even further by promoting individual rights to the point of finding redeeming features in child pornography. Children's rights became a sacrifice to a misinterpretation of the right to freedom of expression, and to the what-next syndrome. Eliminate kiddie-porn with censorship? What next, the Bible and Shakespeare? Only the most determined of voluntary effort in late 20th century affected the balance set by Solzhenitsyn in the 1970s: By what right does the Big Whorehouse assume moral superiority over the Big Gulag?

TIME AND DISTRACTION

Available time is a strange phenomenon. What happens to time gained through relief from long and numbing hours spent at work? In the latter half of the 20th century there was no gain in leisure time, only more time for entertainment.

In ancient Greece and Rome the situation is supposed to have been different, a celebration of the contemplative life. If so, the leisured attention paid religion and philosophy by upper-class men rested upon the backs of slaves who outnumbered them. There was, on the other hand, no equivalent for the modern term "fun." The later experience of democracy has ground down distinctive social-class tastes to a *common* appreciation of entertainment over leisure.

That attitudes toward time changed is more certain than how widespread the 17th-century shift to Weber's Protestant ethic actually was. The Puritans surely endorsed a gospel of work, and tried to enforce it upon the orders below them, but how enthusiastic the latter became about working is open to question. And whoever once might have shared the Puritan compulsion to justify self with disciplined effort at work, that compulsion slackened quite markedly by the latter half of the 20th century.

A clear majority—at least according to those polls—thought they worked too hard. Everyone, notably welfare recipients, had the standard package of things, including a big color TV, so that possessions conferred little envy in the eyes of others. But in a paradoxical way, the felt need to buy more possessions came to "require" the new two-earner marriage. At least that was the advertising message, with its approved future of career women supplanting the housewife, and men as well as women playing cross-gender roles.

It was argued at the time by those more concerned about income levels than the expression of emotions and attitudes that the working wife was created by necessity, that people had to run faster to remain in the same income place. A real *fall* in income was said to be hidden by all those wives who "needed" to work. Such arguments reflected the priorities which had been established.

In either event, intellectuals who wrote about the subject despaired. They said that buying things goaded on the common people, who displayed no interest in contemplative leisure or improving their own taste. Instead those people eagerly sought more commercial recreation and, according to their critics, mindless entertainment.

The common people, to be sure, have always avoided the Finer Things of Life—as have many of their critics. There still remain the better things, the most important of which, to some, is the raising of decent children. The Christian-school movement has proved that the two-earner marriage is unnecessary if husband as well as wife believes that mother-at-home is a more important need than another car, or even any car, that most so-called needs are mere cravings.

A large majority of parents, in late 20th century, deliberately sacrificed time spent with their children in order to buy more things and enjoy non-family distractions. It was widely assumed that the working wife, the two-income family, was the inevitable result of a rising standard of living. That attitude itself was a "problem," encouraging husbands and wives to look upon time spent with their

Relativism and the Family Institution

children as dispensable, as of lesser moment than parties, vacation time away from the kids, and precious uninterrupted hours spent glued to the television set. Hurry ruled most lives, but to get where? Favorite TV programs had a high priority. And possibly one reason why love affairs arrived so quickly in bed was the general lack of enough time for courtship.

A large majority of parents made the critical choice that life is too important to be wasted on one's own children. For individuated hedonists, enough self-sacrifice was already exacted by remaining married and seeing that the minimal physical needs of the children were met. Their reasoning, so far as it went, was correct: doing a proper job with children does seriously impair the opportunity to live one's own life.

As life, for most adults, seemed to be moving faster, a greater number of apparent options in late 20th century opened up, and the fear of closing other doors with every choice, especially that of marriage and family, haunted the imagination. Fear of sacrificing one's potential turned many away from marriage and family, turned them away from irrevocable choice. Such people preferred instead to remain free to choose, until time ran out and there was no one who would mourn.

The relaxation of historic sex roles in housework—by necessity in the two-income case—failed to confer a sense of any extra time upon either partner. Children and hedonistic distractions continued to be incompatible goals. The politicians stood ready to hire willing professional bureaucrats to run large public child-care centers, where children would receive that loving, responsible care for which so many parents could not find the time. They were assured, though, that no crosses or discussion of Christian

The Nature of Morality

principles would be permitted in any of the Child Care programs.

There have been two major explanations for the turn of domestic events in the last quarter of the 20th century. The more ingenious argument, often made, was that a general loss of Christian faith had exacerbated the universal dread of death. With work-time drastically reduced, the millions without philosophic or religious resource were compelled to adopt frenetic time-wasting as the only available defense. Television viewing thus became the most insistent claimant upon the time of all those people who were denied the opportunity to become either contemplatives or heroes.

When people no longer had to work mind-numbing hours by necessity, existential fears plagued those who had no resources to handle them. In such cases the meaning of existence could be confronted only with compulsive distraction. So important did the latter become that the need for more shopping days determined changes in the birthdays of people who were once acclaimed as national heroes. Meanwhile, the frantic step and blank stare were encountered in the streets of smaller towns than New York or Chicago.

Only personal experience of death, as the Puritans knew well, can prepare the emotions for one's own. Instead, avoidance of it became a big industry by the middle of the 20th century, promoted not only by the electronic media but in courses taught at school and colleges. By tacit agreement death was trivialized. Hired professionals helped to combat any ritualization of grief, which became something to overcome as soon as possible, to adjust to. The exercise and vitamin cults more than softened, they denied, the inevitable: "Look and *be* younger every day"! And then there were the new miracle preventives of just about every threat. The people who placed their faith in any of these were not avoiding death at all, only life.

The second major explanation of what happened became quite popular with those who wrote about the American scene at mid-century. The American public was simply transformed into another victim, this time a very big victim. Such an explanation peaked during the 1960s, with the revelations of such people as Marcuse, Leary, and Roszak, when, it was said, everyone was growing up absurd. This particular theme inflated exculpatory rhetoric to the outermost inclusion. The disembodied system was the villain, which created a desire for razor blades over truth. The very success of American capitalism was its own defeat.

So if the path taken was wrong, that was no one's personal responsibility. These writers emulated the social science which was and has remained predominant. In a circle of finger-pointing, responsibility for action taken can never be assigned to the person who acts, but must be shifted to whatever abstract cause rises to prominence. Because they shunt emphasis so rapidly, such explanations are best ignored.

Family Humor

Family humor is an emergent; there was no need for it until status differences within the family came under attack from the outside. What residue of parental authority remains now requires more cajolery, surely much more humor. But it attracts no attention, almost escapes notice.

Family humor is idiosyncratic, and does not translate to others because it is not supposed to be funny to others. This gentlest of all kinds of humor serves to unite people in a close and exclusionary bond, a bond which can be made more secure than all the supposed essential economic functions, the formal patterns and defined statuses, of the past. Family humor is expressed most often in family rituals and celebrations. The foibles and limitations of family others, often and repetitively joked about with no trace of disparagement, makes a circle of common enjoyment.

Such forbearance becomes essential in a family setting more individuated than at any time in the past. Open clashes of interest can no longer be suppressed with overriding authority. Who shall defer to what is "reasonable" and "just" requires from parents a willingness as well as ability to ad lib an absent script. Does the small child have the right to loiter when returning from playtime and endanger her mother's dental appointment? Books have been written on what to do about this and similar situations, books which are of no help because they pass judgment on a general case which does not exist. Each family's idiosyncratic humor, founded in shared love and responsibility, aids in finding a specific answer for particular individuals where there is no general answer.

Paradoxically, as family structure has weakened with a compromising of its traditional functions, the traditional family becomes more, not less, indispensable. In narrowest terms, who will find the time and energy, the patience and willingness, to raise a child when parents choose the easy way out? What politician or bureaucrat will sit up with a strange child who is ill? If not the mother, who else will devote unstinted hours, every day, to keep one weak student on track in his class at school? There are new pressures to indulge Hobbesian impulses, true enough, but only those same individuals can make the moral choice. That choice may lead people to do what they really want to do anyway, but they will do what they want only when they have been trained by like others to do it.

That said, what some may regard as a regression is surely called for when circumstances allow. Some parents have bought a large vegetable plot in order to train their children in habits of personal responsibility. Others have sought out make work to lessen their time spent with outside influences. The uneasiness at doing something without necessity may take some getting used to, but if one cannot change the world at least one can keep one's own corner of it straight. Worth and integrity in the final analysis reside in people, not in ideas. With hard work the family can still be made to take first place in consciousness.

4

RELIGION AS VITAL FORCE

The confrontation over religion is the most fierce and intransigent one now facing America. Much of it comes in disguised form, which is partly the case in the abortion struggle. Much more disguised is a case which at first glance appears much more clear-cut. The contention between evolutionists and creationists, for example, hides even more than it reveals. The creationists err in their belief that the issue is evolution itself, as when an occasional creationist admits the probability that life forms have changed in time. The real issue is the insistence on one side that change in life forms must have occurred by accident, without any possibility that intervening intelligence directed that course. There is, of course, no way that this particular claim, or its rebuttal, can be substantiated.

Another—and in this case permanent—aspect of religion is its intrinsic connection with social class. Tocqueville, for one, identified perpetuation of religious belief with aristocracy, and loss of religion with egalitarian democracy. Since religious belief is now conventionally identified with unenlightened lower-class types, his claim risks a too-ready rejection. What he had in mind was the danger of utopian socialism in egalitarian democracy, where the urge to destroy those who have succeeded is easily aroused.

The Nature of Morality

RELIGION AND SOCIAL CLASS

Relativism, discussed in the previous chapter, dominates our intellectual life and the popular arts. Relativism has been enlisted to sanctify hedonic individuation, the measure of man not even by other men but by the absolute rightness of each person's momentary impulses. Therefore hold no person responsible for whatever he elects to do for *he* is the measure of all things.

Celebration of irresponsibility is accompanied by egalitarian snobbery, an involuted snobbery which can enjoy approval only from the number of unexceptionable people who voice approval of whatever one does. Snobbery of that kind can hardly be relied upon to create any counter movement in the deterioration of social class, because although the purpose of egalitarian snobbery is vanity-power, it cannot aspire to superior conduct—or to elitism as it is called. The impulse to join with others in religious worship is, on the contrary, in part an announcement of superior conduct. In that sense religion is affiliated with social-class expression.

The people who remain faithful to God have a way to measure not only themselves but their surrounding world as well. That is why deeply religious people make poor recruits for socialistic and other utopian schemes. They do not measure their own value by a willingness to become a manipulated tool of faceless social reformers. They know themselves to be an ultimate datum, not something without value in the transitory schemes of other human beings.

As do all other modern radical social reformers, the egalitarian snobs actually vacillate between relativism and absolutism. The behavior of all other peoples, at least those outside the Western orbit, is explained or excused by the application of relativistic standards. They were subjected to basic causes, underlying causes, beyond their control. The American people (egalitarian snobs and defined victims especially excepted) on the other hand embody the abstraction "society." American society is pilloried with responsibility for all that is evil and vicious in the world, especially when some undeveloped (who undeveloped it?) part of it stands opposed to declared American interest.

Christians at one time derived a special pleasure from rescuing victims, acts which redounded to their credit in this world and the next. By contrast, in the modern progressive world credit is assigned to those who are defined as being the victims. In an America perceived as being unfit to live in, moreover, declared Christians have become the chief villains.

Conduct and Standards

Religion, at least when it is not totally watered down and compromised with progressivism, does affirm personal responsibility. Such a standard is the positive aspect of social class. No matter how impoverished the worshiper may be, however inadvertently he may set himself off from all those who fail to measure up, there are some things that he would not do. The intention, of course, falters as often as it is fulfilled, and for religious hypocrites (always in plentiful supply) there is no intention at all. In this connection Auguste Comte argued that without hypocrisy there would be much less formal rectitude.

But good or bad, the professed Christian sends a message which progressives in general and egalitarian snobs in particular find intolerable. The message of superior standards must not only be rejected, it must be defeated.

The Nature of Morality

Church and state must be separated to the point of muting the message, negating it, confining it to a church building and denying it expression any place else. No standard except that which is equally low can escape being sneered at. Even Comte's religious hypocrisy must be denied public expression.

Wealth secured through undisciplined ways and outside the traditional division of labor is alone encouraged in such circles. People who try to succeed in traditional ways are suspect. Especially beyond the pale are those who in one way or another proclaim *moral* conduct which requires effort, and which by its very existence implies that something might be inaccessible to victims defined in such a way as to arouse guilt among traditionalists.

So the message of class and that of religion have become equally resented, for they are rooted in the same impulse: there are some areas where those others are excluded. However compromised by secular and even progressive attitudes religion may have become, such affiliation promotes distinction, the belief that ultimately, as a child of God, each worshiper is freed from the shackles of the idols of the tribe. Acknowledged believers have an open way to resist the socialist or the statist who insist that each integer is part of a vast social problem, equally nothing, only to be handled and directed by those who know best.

That is why Tocqueville found an affinity between aristocracy and religion. Both are inegalitarian, profess or at least imply superior standards. Like each family, they are not accessible to everyone. They practice, at least imply, exclusion. They both provide a permanent tension of resistance to utopian schemes. It is religion, moreover, which stands as the last point of resistance to whatever shifting enthusiasms the majority may espouse.

Assumption of superior standards, self-imposed restrictions to one's own conduct, always contain at least a tinge—even in the case of devoted Christians—of snobbery. And snobbery, like all other aspects of human nature, can both confer and deny. Like every other good, a price must be paid for it. Aristocrats, for example, have exploited women of the lower orders for all of the centuries, as their right, freed from obligation or responsibility. Snobbery granted them an emotional privilege.

Social-class snobbery, on the other hand, can be self-restrictive as well, holding up standards of things which are simply not done by people like us, no matter how deplorably those others may act. Invariably such attitudes have a religious basis. T. E. Lawrence, imbued with Edwardian ideals, exemplified the breed: high scholarship, the seeking of ideal women but never for low purposes, abstinence and self-control, in order to prepare for the duty of leading those of whom much less was expected.

Complexity of Class and Religion

Ultimately, all regulation of impulse provokes contrary forms of behavior, oftentimes within the same person. The religious impulse, although most often associated with social class in terms of holding up moral standards, can also be associated with lowering them. As one instance, for centuries aristocrats, especially the younger ones, have made common if restricted antinomian cause with the lower orders.

Historically, a large proportion of both have lived at and for a present which features creature enjoyment. Both have scorned the respectable middle, who live at the future and are deeply concerned about consequences. The respectable middle, in turn, has always celebrated religion, at least of the formal variety. Here is where striving takes place, something historically rejected by aristocrat and slum-dweller alike.

Aristocracy has been wiped out, mainly by the displacement of social class by the division of labor as the arena where status is won. Since the doctrine of irresponsibility has exempted all non-traditionalists from trying to achieve, defined victims in particular, erstwhile aristocrats—or at least the very rich outside of such unexceptionable areas as professional sports and the entertainment industry—can neither play the T. E. Lawrence role nor that of either Commodore Vanderbilt or Andrew Carnegie. Typically they fund progressive causes, for the guilt now laid upon them exceeds that which has been imposed upon any other segment of the population. That guilt has destroyed their former claim to uphold standards of any kind. Parenthetically, were they to obey a well-known Biblical injunction and raise large families, their wealth would be reduced to near-guiltless dimensions.

RELIGION AND MORALITY

This section addresses two propositions. First, that private morality, the morality of individuals, is the sole determinant of all morality. Second, that the morality of the individual is ultimately dependent upon religious training in the traditional home. To be sure these points, as with the existence of God, cannot be proven by empirical demonstration, but a persuasive case can be made for them.

The Oliners

The ordinarily good man avoids boob-bumping rhetoric, such as any political expression of compassion for the "poor," in which another War on Poverty creates more of it. The most that can be expected of him is what he expects of himself, that he will take care of himself and his family, and of his friends when they may be in real need—and that he will be as honest as he can afford to be with all others. Only the very few dependably good people go further, when they deliberately risk everything.

During the 1964–1965 Eel River Valley flood in Northern California, a few Mennonites arrived among strangers to clean up the mess. They neither sought nor got fanfare, publicity, or TV cameras, and they quietly departed when their work was finished. The Christian rescuers of Jews who were faced with annihilation during the Holocaust was a similar case, if anything a more extreme case, for unlike the Mennonites, they had no backing in official policy. Instead they had to oppose it.

Their story has been told by Samuel P. and Pearl M. Oliner in *The Altruistic Personality* (Free Press, 1988). Their altruism was unaffected by reasoning, although the rescuers did "differ from others in their interpretation of religious teaching and religious commitment . . ." (page 156). They had come to believe, in concrete not theoretical terms, in the common humanity of all people. The rescuers were not people who behaved "virtuously because of autonomous contemplation of abstract principles." In fact "ideology, grand vision, or abstract principles may inure . . . to the suffering of real people" (page 257).

Although the Oliners claim their work supplements the earlier work of Adorno and his group, there is little to link *The Altruistic Personality* to *The Authoritarian Personality*. At the end of World War II the Adorno group announced that religious and traditionalist types veered toward fascism, exemplified the authoritarian personality. At the other end of their scale were self-directed folk without moralistic baggage, who were tolerant and morally autonomous, who arrived at self-transcendence through reason and through values achieved by exploration, who thus became experts at situational ethics. The Oliners tell a very different story, with an equally imposing apparatus of tables and statistical measures.

The people in Germany and the German-occupied territories who rescued individuals from the gas chambers were not Adorno's self-directed non-authoritarians of superior moral insight. Some of them didn't even "like Jews," which is reasonable enough. Any outsider who professes to like some ethnic group is guilty of patronizing impertinence. He can like only his own friends, whatsoever their background may be.

These rescuers—some of whom hid a Jew or Jewish family for two to five years—were not intellectuals or beautiful souls or even interested in politics. Nor were they on the make. To be on the make in either Nazi Germany or Democratic America required going along to get along. The rescuers, in contrast, held to a modest place which stirred no particular envy in others nor any particular aspiration on their part to keep up with or surpass their neighbors.

They made an emotional on-the-spot decision to defy the state, reject public opinion, by deed traduce what their own neighbors espoused, and risk a terrible reprisal, not only upon themselves but also upon the other members of their own families. What led these heroes of morality, without supportive comradeship, to behave far beyond the call of any conceivable duty? Because of the way they were trained as children within the family. It was "the values learned from their parents which prompted and sustained involvement" (page 142).

Each had to see himself as someone who could not live

with himself if *in a personal confrontation* he should reject a fellow human being in desperate need. Such an impulse, contrary as that might sound, was rooted in long, energy-consuming training by religious parents in the ways of conventional morality. Paradoxically, before the impulsive positive act can occur, first must come loving models who induce inhibition with extended hard work of their own.

These findings, dismissed by some as mere common sense, nevertheless move in the direction opposite to what became fashionable in the second half of the 20th century. Freedom of moral choice, the "new morality," ethical relativism, or the autonomous moral individual encouraged to develop his private belief system, do not create the moral hero, not even the ordinarily moral person, whose morality, to repeat, denotes principled restrictions to his own conduct, restrictions accepted before a decision to act is formed. The rescuers rose far above that negative standard.

No one can predict when or where the moral hero will appear. The Oliners show that he becomes possible only when his life has been enmeshed in close relationship with moral others. That is a requirement for producing even the ordinarily moral person. There is a parallel here with Durkheim's work on suicide in the West. He concluded that extremely low rates occur inversely with the extent of individuation.

In the Oliners' sample, 406 rescuers, 126 nonrescuers (those who rejected pleas for help), and 108 survivors of the Nazi persecution were interviewed in depth. All Gentiles who hid Jews and helped them to escape when possible are estimated by the Oliners to number into the thousands. A small minority, to be sure, but still far more numerous than progressive thought would admit—if progressive thought could imagine the issue.

After the War the rescuers' moral life continued, albeit on a less heroic scale. The old trait-versus-situation argument would appear to have been settled by solid evidence. Faced with the "same situation," many, many more people turned their backs. But of course this, and similar evidence, in late 20th century changed little of consequence, for such evidence failed to support fashionable thought and challenged too many powerful interests.

Professor Edward O. Wilson

In the reductionist outlook, exemplified by Professor Wilson, the Oliners' examination of human nature is sheer poppycock. He scorns all journals of opinion for purveying inexact terms, for not using statistics and mathematics. Professor Wilson expresses total conviction in his *On Human Nature* (Harvard, 1978) that "pure [reductionist] knowledge is the ultimate emancipator" (page 96). He apparently overlooks the possibility that there may be an inherent opposition between exact answers and significant questions.

This father of sociobiology echoes Margaret Mead: "we" must plan, in this case for a future based upon scientific materialism. We have had enough of historical anecdotes, "diachronic collating of outdated, verbalized theories of human behavior," judgments governed by "personal ideology" and a lot of effervescence (page 203). Given the precise answers of molecular biology, a breeding program should be instituted to rectify such errors. This program must of course be controlled, not by legislators but by biological experts, within, to be sure, a democratic context.

This program, over the centuries, will produce a population more tolerant than now of racial differences, of feminism and of gay rights. "All that we can surmise of humankind's genetic history argues for a more liberal sexual morality . . ." (page 142). And so the "traditional Judeo-Christian view of homosexual behavior is inadequate and probably wrong" (page 146).

Unfortunately, some people may prove to be reluctant to breed as directed by democratic means. For one thing, religion appears to have a hold upon many who may not be able to take their scientific materialism neat. For them "we" will create new myths about evolution, indeed a new religion. But Professor, with or without a new religion, each individual will always regard himself as an ultimate datum, never as nothing but a temporary repository of genes who thinks only of a distant future of improved biology.

There is something else out of joint here, and that is the temporary conjuncture of perceived interests which rules social life. The pieties of any present, enshrined in slogans, do not last, as any reading of an old newspaper will make clear. Ideological slogans change much faster than the centuries required to study the effects of a human breeding program. More critically, what does genetics have to do with preferences governed by prejudice? What do the specific targets of prejudice have to do with genetics when the targets shift rapidly in time?

Parsons

Talcott Parsons in his *Structure of Social Action* (McGraw-Hill, 1937) defined positivism in a way far different from that employed by Auguste Comte, and by most of those who followed Comte. For Parsons, positivism is the mistaken notion that man forever seeks a "scientific" explanation for his own dilemmas, the mistaken notion that any failure to find one can only result from ignorance or error. He says that an alternative view is that of a "reality" which is "significant to human life and experience, yet outside the range of scientific observation and analysis" (page 421).

It is this reality, says Parsons, that in a shared means-ends schema builds from the cares of ordinary existence to "ultimate ends" of morality and especially of religion. A "solidarity of individuals" requires a unity of allegiance to a common body of moral rules (page 389). Shared ultimate ends, not private ends, hold a people together and maintain order. Parsons does fail to explain why one set of ultimate ends, or collective pieties, can be superseded in many particulars, but that was not his purpose.

The present discussion does, though, depart from Parsons' vision of order as a universally-shared experience to one maintained, at least in civilization, by one part of a population. He assumed a common involvement in means-ends schemas which are crowned by a fusing of goals and purposes. By ignoring how suppression has imposed compliance to the goals of others throughout history, Parsons achieved a markedly democratic world view.

The people discussed above make a case for the indispensability of religion in maintaining morality—albeit Wilson inadvertently. Social life, then, is (or was in the immediate past) grounded in religion, but no religion can serve its necessary function without a presumption of truth, unless it is literally accepted, is never approached as a prescription drug. Religion as therapy, however, has come to characterize modern organized religion, whether in good or bad faith.

THE SOCIAL ISSUES

Social problems persist because progressive solutions demand an acceptable context, which includes an absolute ban on suppression in any degree. This horror of suppression is a matter of unknowing, or indifference, to the bewildered majority. Nor does either side understand that when one is seeking, as is invariably the case, to define underlying and basic causes of problems, all other problems must be simultaneously "solved" in order to solve the particular focus of attention. Thus those who seek to solve problems are as bewildered, surely as helpless, as the majority, for unlike the majority they perceive an ideal world where no price is ever paid and no trade-off demanded. This world they perceive is beyond the ken of the majority, who oftentimes define as problems one or another thing dismissed as ridiculous by progressive problem-solvers.

Many of the progressive problem-solvers promote the major interests of the professional humanitarian industry, such as the "problem of the homeless." Traditionalists would "solve" it by forcing the mentally-physically able to go to work, reinstitutionalize the mental cases, and take care of the motivated indigent. But when one is striving to indict "society" for its cruelty and heartlessness, such a "solution" is anathema, especially to those who stand to profit from a bureaucracy expanding to meet created need. And this crusade, of course, is profitable in emotional as well as material terms.

The two problems discussed below are different. They are without specific history, having persisted since before the record began, and they are perceived by progressive and traditionalist alike as problems, albeit not with the same emphasis. These problems express the tragic and ineradicable gulf between moral aspiration and animal reality. And unlike the case of the homeless "problem," the majority, the common people, hold definite and passionate opinions about both pornography and abortion.

They are engaged, they believe they can make a difference. And these issues are an integral part of a universal religious imperative, which most so-called social problems are not. These issues are also affiliated with social-class expression, in the sense that both sides are quite aware of inclusion-exclusion and a social-class kind of affirmation of moral superiority—clear in the case of abortion, much less so in the case of pornography.

Pornography and abortion are still ideologically attuned, even though abortion, in expressed opinion, has many more progressive defenders than does pornography. Positions on both issues are formed by the same opposed perceptions of human nature and the world. Both issues may possess a history that goes back to the start of the record, but only since the 1960s have progressives invoked the power of law for protection of both, with an ensuing conflict of racking bitterness. In this conflict most progressives may declare pornography to be personally offensive, but when they confront traditionalists on what should be done about it, they opt for legally-protected hedonic individuation. The ogre of *legal* suppression, even in the modest guise of censoring pornography, is one the progressive sensibility cannot stomach.

Pornography

There is one salient difference between the two issues: only in the case of pornography is everyone unavoidably and personally involved. The reason goes much deeper than the ubiquity of the stuff, once available only under the counter or mailed in a plain brown wrapper. What offends the modern public is the open and invasive display of a degradation they wish would remain dormant in imagination. Because of the attraction to the secret self of invasive pornography, no one can find an escape from a steady coarsening of sensibility. It is here that moral commitment to religious-familial restrictions meets a pervasive challenge, the delusion of an orgiastic future. Publicly expressed revulsion is in part an answer to the need for self-protection.

A vast majority of citizens overtly opposed pornography. According to Mr. Gallup, over 90 percent of them felt deeply offended by it, yet pornography became legally nonpornographic. An equal proportion did not want any public display of pornographic magazines. Commercial purveyors of pornography, nevertheless, were cleared to continue while the majority were held hostage.

For the progressive elite, courts became the favored refuge, where majority opinion went unregistered. The government which ruled may have been permissive, but it was not a democracy, at least not in the sense of responsiveness to the will of the people. The will of the people, as always however, was at odds with itself. Not only did elected officials profess shock at pornography and then did nothing for fear of offending special constituencies, they also pacified the public with those unconnected special favors demanded by this or that part of it. In defense of elected officials, it should be pointed out that they were hobbled by a self-perpetuating bureaucracy and a seemingly independent judicial process (both of which they encouraged), as well as by a self-divided public.

There is less defense for one argument used by the progressive elite: if the door to pornography were held

The Nature of Morality

wide open, then people would become bored and turn away. A considerable majority are really attracted by it, an attraction which measures their revulsion. And on the supply side there can be only a continuous exploration of previously forbidden territory. There is a need to take another step, for commercial reasons to invade what is still deemed inviolable.

Freedom of expression, the raised holy chalice of the First Amendment, held back democratic majorities, which included most progressives if not the progressive elite. How could the cultural sewer have been deepened and widened in opposition to what most Americans finally wanted? Even the massive drift toward progressivism, which dragooned whatever opinion balked at a particular sensitive issue, does not explain the hopelessness of majority affirmation when, as in this instance, it confronted the law. The progressive elite made no bones about their determination to make over America in their own image, and their gathering success could only be explained as an exercise in effective power.

In addition there was no place where people of like mind on an issue of conscience could get together, especially when their perceived material interests took them in many different directions. In majority opinion, something may be dreadfully wrong, but the unorganized troops cannot be marshaled to move in a single direction. The more people who are involved on any such issue, the less can they repair to anything like a Town Meeting, so that strategically located minorities—here a few ACLU lawyers—can dictate policy.

Procedural legal absolutism rode the majority, another illustration of the principle that the few always rule, no matter what the formal designation of government may be. Still, as is usually the case, the villains escaped precise identification. By late 20th century the legislative branch of government had handed over pornography, abortion, and similar "family issues" to the courts, a bonanza for progressive activism. Congress, with a relief shared by the executive branch, could refer this or that outraged constituency to the court system, and judges ruled on such issues as what is a family, on rent control, on what local school boards could do, and on what local tax rates must be.

Glittering words, such as Democracy, can in time change whatever the referent once was while retaining sentimental attraction. But the little that was left in late 20th century of earlier habit and conviction still provided traditionalists with a way out. Within the cultural sewer recalcitrants could escape to the family with like-minded others, and try to build what Koestler called cultural islands, in the hope that their descendants would have a better place in which to create a life.

Abortion

Unlike the case of pornography, there was no near unanimity on the abortion issue. The adversaries were about equally divided for many years following the *Roe* v. *Wade* Supreme Court ruling of 1973, that abortion is legal and laws to the contrary in thirty-one states are unconstitutional. That ruling was based on every woman's "right to privacy," which in effect stated that a fetus is not a person under the Constitution, and thus has no right to life.

But long before *Roe* v. *Wade* the fetus had no security. Religion did not confer it in the 17th century; neither has anything else ever since. Abortion is an ancient theme. What became new in the last quarter of the 20th century was an impassioned political confrontation on the subject.

The Nature of Morality

Here were two ultimate claims upon human sentiment and identification, irreconcilably in conflict. What was at stake was the tortuous question, the ultimate question, of what is the meaning of human life. The "right of a woman to control her own body" confronted the perception that those bodies weren't being at all controlled and that 1.7 million babies were being murdered every year. A zero-sum game of opposed humanitarian claims was being played: to protect innocent victims of rape and incest (the ploy of citing the exceptional case as the norm) on one side, to prevent a slaughter of the innocents on the other.

Behind all else lay progressive vs. traditionalist loyalties, which were not clearly registered at the fringes of polled response. It has been demonstrated that on this and most other issues, the polls can get any majority desired by asking the appropriate question. Polled majorities don't like "abortion on demand," but majorities will also endorse every woman's right "to control her own body." Actually, the way the question is posed gets the floating answer: about three-fourths of American adults oppose the reasons why nearly all abortions are now obtained—convenience or belated contraception.

The polls also indicate a great deal of popular confusion about what is legally allowed and forbidden. The issue is often posed as one of making certain that abortion is not declared to be illegal. There is not the slightest danger of such a restriction being imposed. If *Roe* v. *Wade* were declared to be unconstitutional, the various individual states would continue to legislate the matter, as they did prior to 1973. Again, there is a popular myth that legal abortion cannot be performed except in the first three months of pregnancy. *Roe* v. *Wade* permitted abortion during every month of a woman's pregnancy, and the last recorded Supreme-Court ukase would permit abortion until the fetus is viable.

The people who made opposed humanitarian claims were not polled majorities but doctrinaire progressives and traditionalists. On one side was the ascendant insistence that each person is responsible only to and for himself (a position which should not be confused with an affirmation of self-autonomy). On the other was the belief that encouragement of hedonic individuation could only further erode a sense of obligation to those who will replace us, those in a critical sense yet unborn. But neither side was really engaged in debate; both wanted to dragoon public opinion in their own direction, to threaten authority with disruption, as did the civil-rights marchers of the early 1960s, who faced solid majorities who had told pollsters the civil-rights movement had gone "too far."

Meanwhile the debate, so far as it holds relevance, continues. For traditionalists, supporters of abortion on demand beg a lot of questions. Do a minor girl's parents or the abortionist have the right to guide her choice? Should the husband be denied control of his own body when he opposes his wife's decision to abort? What about an unborn child's legal right to inherit property? Except in extremely rare cases, every pregnant woman volunteered, at least to run the risk of becoming so, and in that perspective her decision to abort strains any appeal to the abstract sentiment of "freedom of choice."

On the other hand, the pro-lifers have been accused of promoting the birth of unwanted babies, and then of denying personal responsibility for the loving care, warm meals, monitored health, and the like, required by those unwanted babies. The point is both justified and beside the point. What the pro-lifers perceive in imagination is a renewal of respect for human life, a world where babies

The Nature of Morality

will be wanted and cared for. It is doubtful that this desire could be gratified by "returning the issue to the individual states," by forcing determined women to go to some other jurisdiction to get aborted. Like other family affirmations, this one is self-fulfilling. If enough will could be affirmed to resist government-sanctioned abortion, then the institution of the family would to that extent have already recovered.

The souls of Americans were deeply perplexed. Large majorities of those who were polled would deny use of abortion as delayed contraception, would prohibit abortion if the unborn child were not the desired sex, or if parents would be left uninformed about the abortion of their minor child. This restriction of parental control was later, cautiously, amended.

It was only after the Supreme Court prohibited the various states from legislating the question of abortion that the right-to-life movement, which included Catholics, Jews, Protestants, and agnostics as well, was formed. As for the committed fundamentalists and evangelicals, they had never been stirred to political action unless the protection of children was at issue. In their view that protection had been surrendered to the Devil when a third of all babies conceived in this country were being killed *with legal sanction* before they ever met the mysteries of self awareness, of the world, and of God.

The media favored abortion: 97 percent of Hollywood's TV people in 1983 supported it. But before indignation over that fact is aroused, or over the brutal dismissal of a "blob of protoplasm," or even about the estimated 1.7 million abortions legally performed every year in this country, the traditionalists must consider that before *Roe v. Wade* there were an estimated 1 million abortions, legal and illegal. Effective demand for the service operates regardless of the legal status of the supply. Still, as in the case of pornography, the sticking point is not the persisting fact of abortion—whether legal or illegal the practice will continue, as the pro-abortionists correctly aver—but official sanction of the practice which, to the militant anti-abortionist, signifies an *imposed* abandonment of restraint amidst the world's decay. The absolute demand for personal rights has made law—not religion, not community, not the family—the ultimate authority.

This is one issue which most definitely will never be settled once and for all. Arguments about when life begins fail to address the question about what the meaning of life might be. And so the slide into the use of aborted tissue purchased in order to "save lives" is an issue our descendants will have to confront. But the question of what life means will never go away, even though the instrumental attitude toward it could intensify, at least for a while.

The touching faith of so many Americans in communication or "dialogue" is in this context revealed as a mirage. Here is the ultimate confrontation, where traditionalist and progressive face each other across an echoless chasm, because human beings are finally emotional instead of being rational creatures. As for the insistence upon guarding parenthood, however reluctant that parenthood in many cases might be, a famous musician once said when asked what he was trying to do with his trumpet: If you need to ask, you'll never get to know.

The Confused Laity

These sexual issues are uncertainly being addressed from the pulpit. Pastor Neuhaus, for one, declared the public square abandoned in sexual matters by the churches and

The Nature of Morality

other once character-building agencies to the popular mechanics of sex. Parental disapproval wavered. The notion that potentially "sexually active" youngsters can be rescued from the danger of contracting venereal diseases only with condoms and clean needles, by technical means alone and not with moral instruction, became the only publicly-acceptable control. The sequence of events was circular: incite others to irresponsible behavior, and then use the consequences to justify further incitement to the same behavior, because they're going to do it anyway.

The churches, by and large, had little in the way of moral instruction to offer, the established Protestant churches less than the Catholic. Mainline pastors feared that the Ten Commandments would offend their congregations. Many of them so admitted. Instead of zinging away at Original Sin, they dithered about sex, such as referring to it as God's gift to man, which to young ears provided little reason for waiting to try it. Substantially abandoned by the churches, the young had only the family left for whatever help they could get in avoiding the public square.

That public square featured the taboos of the new morality, including any negative reference to official feminism, any attempt to describe racial or ethnic-group differences, any discussion of AIDS which noted homosexual responsibility, and use of anything in the Bible to explain human conduct. Given an audience most of whom had been cowed into submission for fear of being considered quaint or out-of-date, samizdat could rarely be circulated. The result displayed a profound misapprehension of human nature.

Bewildered parents were promised that if outmoded and vicious Victorian-puritanical restraints were removed, their kids would only do what comes naturally, and a blessed dawn of freedom and loving compassion would arrive, loving compassion being demonstrated by the act of putting on a condom. There also was the anthropological evidence presented in studies of the Wanga-Wangas, who never practice libidinal restraint. Apparently any Wanga-Wanga determination to improve their own lousy living conditions petered out many centuries ago.

The preachers themselves are seeking one apologetic substitute for God after another, such as political activism, therapy, or social work. So long as they do they will continue to lose their congregations. They have been sliding into positivism, looking for the reality behind the facade. But until they cease turning away from the simple faith that God is, their congregations will continue to fade away and they will remain essentially irrelevant in the moral struggle.

MODERN GNOSTICISM

Has a new religion, a New Age religion, emerged in the modern world? Surely—if strange practices and lots of noise define a real situation. To be sure there is more than that, for powerful bureaucracies within the mainline churches, along with trendy clerics, flirt with rejection of their received doctrine in favor of some variant of self-celebration. The basis of the religious impulse is the urge to live beyond our fingertips; as such, it remains vulnerable to enthusiasm for novelties.

Historically, the deviation from orthodoxy, from God defined as clearly other, has often embraced an unsophisticated version of Gnosticism, in which heaven, hell, and God are all located within the self. In such cases usually, although not always, votaries have been encouraged to reject all conventional restrictions on sexual license. The

Anabaptists of the 16th century degenerated into the Kingdom of Zion with its holy promiscuity. It was a similar sexual Gnosticism which emerged in late 20th century.

Not all counterfeit religions are Gnostic nor do they of necessity celebrate irresponsible sex. Marxism and the faith in progress have claimed incalculably more adherents. All counterfeit religions, Gnostic or not, do, however, fulfill two major functions of religion: they justify individual suffering and they enhance the feeling of self-importance.

Marxism provides a fairly good counterfeit. All suffering is caused by evil capitalists who, once destroyed, will cease causing the world's misery. As for self-importance, it offers a sacred text, many saints, redemption of a sort, and the end of history. Such a combination of emotional satisfactions cannot be destroyed by the "failure of socialism."

It was in late 18th century France that another non-Gnostic substitute for God, a faith in progress, reached a greater popularity among an intellectual minority than did Marxism later. Counterfeit religions which are not Gnostic provide a smoother transition from what is already accepted. Tradition is much less flouted, in fact for intellectuals the transition can be easy.

An American historian, Carl Becker, in his *The Heavenly City of the Eighteenth Century Philosophers* (Yale, 1932) has pointed out that his subjects were mistaken in their claim to be the great destroyers of the medieval myth. They called themselves rationalists and ridiculed the idea that the earth had been made in six days, *but* they perceived their world as a beautifully articulated machine made for man by a Supreme Being. They denounced the Church and the Bible, *but* they worshiped the authority of Nature and Reason. They scoffed at the Garden of Eden, *but* they depicted primitive man as a Noble Savage, the product of living in a golden age of Roman virtue. They denied the Biblical miracles, *but* they proclaimed their faith in human progress and human perfectibility. And so "the *Philosophes* demolished the Heavenly City of St. Augustine only to rebuild it with more up-to-date materials" (page 31). Still, while one minority or another may be convinced they are shifting the scenery, human nature abides.

Ideal And Practice

What also abides is a persistence through the centuries of those who strive to live according to what they know is right. Although man is a complex creature, riven by contradictory impulses, there have always been those individuals who strive to live according to the highest religious ideal, while many more of their fellows gouge and connive their way through their own lives. Other men, who refuse to pursue the highest religious ideal, yet long for moral wholeness, strive to keep the ideal alive while they regret their own shortcomings. The existence of an ideal thus has important consequences for behavior, no matter how many men fail to live up to it.

The continued existence of the highest religious ideal, the desire for it, the striving toward it, all directly affect whatever level of proximate justice and charity any community and its religious organizations are capable of achieving. If a lofty peak of religious aspiration were not described, *as an ideal*, by those very religious organizations which, as organizations, cannot scale it, then the life about us would be visited by more cruelty, hatred, double-dealing manipulation, and sin than it now contains. This line of thought has implications for those "scientists" who have insisted that since human sexual behavior falls short of all religious and ethical ideals, then the sexual standard should be reduced to operating practice.

Holding to received faith identifies the votary and his God. Organized religion, on the other hand, has always stammered, always entertained political aspirations in *this* world. The false prophets warned against in the New Testament have been at work ever since the first Christians gathered at the home of one of their fellows. But assumed basic and underlying causes can be ignored, since the itch to inject politics into Christianity has bothered many churchmen themselves.

Other churchmen accepted scientific explanations for natural occurrences, despite the clear note of moral determinism which resounds throughout the Bible, and thus avoided the knowledge that love for and praise of God rejects the ancient problem of unfilled moral determinism. While 19th-century Christians overwhelmingly remained faithful to received doctrine, the men behind the pulpit started the drift toward invoking "science says" as the ultimate authority. Only for a while did religious capitulation stop at the point where the reality of the supernatural world might be questioned. As noted below, the new pressure now being exerted by some men of the cloth is to deny received faith.

The Modern Situation

Even that drift has failed to quell the main argument over the religiosity of the American people. Ninety percent of them, when polled, declare that they "believe in God." If so, God restricts their lives about as much as a trendy cleric. One trendy cleric, the Rev. Joseph Fletcher, Professor of Ethics, Episcopal Theological Seminary, Cambridge, Massachusetts, emerged during the sixties at a time when authority in both university and church body collapsed in craven surrender. He announced that "unmarried love could be infinitely more normal than married love." Sex is right or wrong depending upon what it does for each person. Morality thus becomes solely a matter of ideological commitment, not of rules external to the self, not at all of a God external to the self. His kind of mischief, widely shared by others like him, had many sources, one of which was his failure to recognize that his own careful inhibitions were not shared by most of those who eagerly followed his advice.

His situational ethics—what is right in one situation may be wrong in another—he placed under the control of each person's independent "value structure." Such freedom by the like-minded people who followed him celebrates a compassion for defined victims, to be sponsored by the state and paid for by all those who are not ornately compassionate. The next step, in religious terms, was worship of the self, a return to the Gnostic faith of the early Christian era without its thought structure and accepted restrictions.

Obviously, no church can be erected on such a foundation. And oddly enough, self-worship has accompanied a cheapening of the value placed upon human life. Euthanasia, suicide, abortion, have become endorsed by precisely the same social types which have turned to self-worship, and perhaps not so oddly. The cheapening of life on one hand and self-worship on the other express in common a revulsion against ordered living in the ultimate expression of relativism.

At this time organized Christianity is more threatened by the insistence upon secular compassion than by neo-

Gnosticism. There has been a massive shift within the Church, Catholic as well as Protestant, from faith in God to faith in social service. That is the main reason why the number of young men and women who are prepared to devote their lives as priests and nuns has fallen drastically in recent decades. If Christ is no longer central, then what is the mission? There is little the modern religious can gain by travelling to foreign countries in order to apologize for the influence of Western culture.

The bureaucrats busy within the various Protestant denominations are much more progressive than their Catholic opposite numbers. The itch to overturn whatever once was has led some of them to claim that God cannot be a white male (who ever made that assertion?) but only a black or even "she," who astonishingly resembles the Earth Goddess. In like vein, for its assigned Bible readings, in late 20th century the National Council of Churches retranslated "Jesus" from the "Son of Man" to the "Human One." God's revelation of himself then becomes patent fiction, constructed by the human authors to gain power over others: traditional God masks a state of false consciousness. The National Council thus parades the fallacious assumption that the fads of the moment will (as well as should) permanently uproot sacred texts and practices. The National Council might be answered as Stalin should have been when he asked how many divisions does the Pope have: the Pope is still there.

Secular compassion and neo-Gnosticism thus move in tandem. The danger of the latter, sometimes referred to as New Age, stems from the desperate hunger to be relieved of all personal responsibility, so that only others can be guilty of victimizing those chosen as surrogates for one's own insistence upon self-importance. As always, however, those who retain their Christian faith can be certain that their own worth is not hostage to the envisioned triumph of one social order or another.

The *declared* forms of New Age Gnosticism spread little confusion compared with the dominance of New Age sensibility within the Catholic as well as Protestant bureaucracy. The bureaucrats, in turn, have been set on course by the mainline divinity schools. Fundamentalist congregations know exactly what is going on, so they steer their own future ministers to the few schools which are not designed to rob them of their faith, to substitute for Christianity social welfare and other political causes.

Paul Tillich, whose work of the fifties became a feature in mainline divinity schools, called for "absolute faith" in the "God above God." This God he defined as "the basic and universal symbol for what concerns us ultimately." But Tillich, a transitional figure, did not believe that a traditional Christian who has neither matured nor achieved sophistication should be informed that his faith is only symbolically and not literally true.

New Age Gnosticism has also made considerable progress in the public-school system. By convinced or frightened teachers, hints about Christian faith are banned in excess of legal requirements. Much more so than in the modern church, secular explanations and secular mythology have replaced God, the Bible, even marriage and what was once viewed as the normal family. The joys of individuated consumerism and of state collectivism are much more openly declared goals there than they are in any except a very few modern churches.

It is fortunate that we do not march through history. False starts and reversals of emphasis, and then a return to earlier anomalies, are much more characteristic of the record. Human nature has always been capable of overturning received wisdom, and will so remain. Gnosticism,

Witches' Sabbaths, and the rest of it have showed up in every century. The only possibly new aspect of modern fake religion is a reduction in the proportion of official people, especially authority figures, who feel safe enough and sure enough to point out how sterile and hopeless the "latest" form of religious enthusiasm is.

Christianity has been encroached upon somewhat more than in other recent centuries by those who can find truth only in identity, in self-creation. Since in their outlook all of reality serves only subjective truth in a power struggle, it does not really matter whether Africans discovered America before Columbus or whether Columbus was the agent of a vicious white conspiracy. Facts, logic, any traditional received wisdom, are all chimeras. Modern Gnosticism thus becomes another variant of atheism—wildly progressive, demanding rejection of the hope that the church has something to tell us about how we should live. But as St. Augustine pointed out, those who dismiss God will never know what kind of creature man is.

5

SOCIAL CLASS AND PREJUDICE

Even though they are more negative than positive, pictures in the mind which dominate perception of the world and the people in it are not errors to be corrected. Negative pictures may be modified in time only to return with a new generation, or the pictures may single out a substitute target group. In either event, we never deal with a problem, that is, something to be corrected in time, but with a condition of permanent reality.

SNOBBERY AND HIGHER EDUCATION

The proposition that we (whoever we might be) are better than those others (whoever they might be) is one that imposes discord upon the body politic, but it can also confer harmony. In one context snobbery presents cruel rejection, in another it upholds standards. For centuries higher education, for example, served to accentuate the gap between us and them, in standards of rectitude as well as scholarship. The people outside were exempted from those standards. They were excused for any failure to measure up; they were expected to follow different, and lower, interests. Here as elsewhere, it should be noted, the battle was never won. A love for learning and obedience to principled restrictions were as often as not treated sullenly by young aristocrats seeking another patina of distinction, and instrumentally by people on the make, middling aspirants to professional employment, especially the ministry. Both social types did, though, arrive on campus with some rudiments of a cultured background which, as Jacques Barzun has pointed out, must begin at the mother's knee.

The men they faced behind the desk at the turn of the century were mostly hacks, as always prunes and prisms. Still, at prestigious institutions there was an opportunity to converse with real scholars in either playful or serious mood. At Harvard, for example, students could sit with William James and Santayana, even meet the chief administrator, Charles William Eliot. What these men notably possessed was an independent stake in the social order which insulated them from the political process. They were not on the make, and could not be intimidated by people outside their own shop.

They were freed of any anxiety to avoid career landmines in what they said and wrote, nor did they accept any pressure to bend their opinions to the wind of the moment. They were not craven upstarts, who at one time would sign loyalty oaths and welcome an FBI agent investigating a student suspected of expressing radical opinions, at another time vote to drop required classical writers from the curriculum in favor of evanescent but trendy reputations.

James, Santayana, and Eliot were not for sale. Their unreflective integrity of mind and character has many conceivable explanations, but an upper-class position protected them from coercion. The paradox of inequality and freedom they made explicit. Only class can obviate that enslavement to public opinion which Tocqueville saw as the special handicap of democracy. This permanent intrin-

Social Class and Prejudice

sic relationship between class and learning was recognized by all of the ancient writers as well as by most of the modern ones down to recent times.

When classes still existed, as in the later 19th century, a few obscure Judes were passionately attracted to Greek and Latin as certified badges of inclusion of some kind. When, as later happened, higher education became a vested right for everyone without regard for means, capability, interest, or even intellectual curiosity, when higher education became a vested right to be "given," knowledge was spat out by those who could be given only a degree. The inestimable flood of such conferred degrees fed the reservoir of egalitarian hatred for learning, exemplified on TV where the villain is often identified by the shelved books which frame his machinations.

It should be kept in mind that the liberal arts, what are known as the humanities, are alone under consideration. Late 20th-century youngsters who were committed to achievement usually attended technical schools attached to the colleges and universities, such as forestry, business, fisheries, agriculture, engineering, and the like. They and their mentors usually worked hard in an atmosphere relatively free of contention and pathologies. They tended to be less bothered by the postures of the moment than were liberal-arts people.

Ideological traditionalists disagree on when it was that the liberal arts suddenly deteriorated, because they deteriorated not long after the complainant was himself in college. At any rate, the previously slow deterioration in higher education seems to have worsened immediately following World War II. General Omar Bradley at that time told an assemblage of university presidents that they had better forget their qualms about admitting people under the GI Bill who lacked the proper credentials. With the lure of all those dollars, they complied. Then began the great slide toward making the university available to outside politics and politicians. Indeed the protectors of the great tradition themselves became politicians, whose gravest public concern about forty years later descended to the level of: "Tell us what you want us to say, and we'll say it."

Before that level was reached the university, and the college, took intermediate steps to make themselves more accessible. The most consequential decision made was the one to welcome research subsidies from foundations and government. Outside bureaucrats could then determine lines of thought and censor potential lines of criticism in a subtle way. The overriding question for ambitious academics became: "What do they want?"

By the 1960s colleges and universities had become dumping grounds for social-reform promotion, political activism, transitory fads, institutes for vested interests, and concern about everyone's psychic welfare, especially about that of the undergraduate. He was invited to participate in planning courses. By the 1980s egalitarianism decreed on most campuses that students be invited to grade their instructors' performance. Why not? By what right do professors grade students if students in turn cannot grade them? The difference was that professors were not informed about how they themselves were being graded. Students' grades improved dramatically.

In 1960 there were six first-generation collegians for every one whose father had attended college. Twenty years later students were nevertheless expected to arrive on campus with knowledge about what they wanted to learn and how they should be taught. Essential authority virtually collapsed.

Authority should not be confused with authoritarianism, as it often is. If learning is to retain even a vestige of meaning, the essential relationship between instructor and student remains one of authority, authority vested in the instructor's status *only* as a consequence of his presumed superior knowledge of a particular subject which the student is assumed, however massive the contrary evidence, to be motivated to study. That kind of authority cannot be maintained in an atmosphere of egalitarian camaraderie, where egalitarian opinion rules.

Ideas do have consequences, but not so compelling consequences as those of perceived interest. The more competent professors fled to research, foundation grants, graduate-student thesis committees—anything to get them out of a classroom where they lacked authority. That the loss was largely self-inflicted is beside the hypocritical point. The loss of authority in academia, whoever was to blame, became much worse than in, say, the family or government or church, or in any division of labor off the campus. It was in the halls of learning, not in factory or office, where rational discourse was supplanted by mindless visceral slogans that would have shamed an intelligent child.

There were professors, and the number is unknown, who first encouraged, then tolerated, then fled, the outburst of apocalyptic passion which bored, frustrated, goalless trend-setters on campus felt safe enough to incite. These people were not primarily on the make but seekers of revenge upon an outer world which would neither solve their personal problems nor say no to their tantrums. But the magic helper, the indulgent tyrant who would let them do what they wanted and tell them what to do, failed to appear. Meanwhile, in any generic sense the university had virtually ceased to be an institution.

In the very late 20th century an even more dismal script

The Nature of Morality

unfolded. Students who had drifted with revolt during the 1960s then made up the most vociferous of faculty members. These were people who had no personal knowledge of the world outside the classroom, who had been sheltered by parents and then continued their sheltered life from AB to PhD and then to tenure. What the new professoriate really wanted was not so much social reform as tenure, advancement, much higher salaries, and beyond these considerations, to be finally vindicated. They could feel vindicated because the ideologies they and some of their own professors had espoused, which coalesced in egalitarian snobbery, became regnant policy when administrators endorsed them.

These ideologies bore several names, the most prominent being cultural Marxism and deconstructionism. Proponents of the latter tried to demonstrate that the revered books which have come down from the past, the "canon" in their jargon, actually were a masquerade. They covered a sinister plot to propagandize the values of DWEM, or Dead White European Males, which included racism, capitalism, Christianity, and patriarchy—with its penchant to make war. For the academic radicals communication with outsiders was assumed to be impossible, since the texts in the canon had no determinative meanings except for their propaganda content. The deconstructionist challenge was meant to reveal that content for what it really was.

Deconstructionists deny that the demonstrable worth of an idea can be only presumptively affected by the background of the proponent. Ideas instead directly reflect identity. Recall the old argument, popular with Freudian analysts, that only Freudians can understand Freud. Thus with deconstructionists only women can understand abortion or appreciate sexual harassment, and only blacks can understand white prejudice. White men, alive or dead, cannot be trusted to comment upon sex or race. So all interpretations, it might be assumed, can be equally valid or invalid. That is not quite the case. Deconstructionists, like all determinists, reject the opinion that their own opinions might have been determined. Their own interpretations are true.

Cultural Marxism and deconstructionism conceal as much as they proclaim. Loyalty to the Third World appears to be of primary concern, and the ultimate villain is America, for all its collective crimes. When the assembled faculty of the university which is arguably number one or two in national prestige voted to drop some classical authors in favor of writers who were "women and minorities," they had the blessing of the administration. Shortly thereafter students paraded the campus shouting "Hey, Hey, Ho, Ho, Western Culture's Gotta Go!" The difficulty, as Professor Bernard Lewis pointed out at the time, was that anything to substitute for Western culture went unmentioned. It was only in the rest of the contemporary world that polygamy, slavery, torture, starvation, and unlimited government were lavishly available, if not uniformly so. The rest of the world, though, affirmed freedom from any interest in alien cultures, an interest which is unique to the West.

If comparison retains any justification at all, in Africa, Asia, and the Middle East was enforced a racism far more severe than anything known in the United States, and the same goes for "the subjugation of women." Traditionalists often blamed college students for this dissonance of thought, but those students had been taught what to think before they arrived on campus. The New York City Board of Education, for example, in its resource guide for the public schools insisted that Chief Sitting Bull henceforth must be known as Totanka Iotanka, and advised that women should be illustrated in texts as being taller than any accompanying man. Again, in the 1960s Eldridge Cleaver's *Soul on Ice* was made required reading in most high schools. His later *Soul on Fire*, written after he had spent some time in the Third World, in which he recanted his earlier expression of loathing for the United States, was not. What is involved here is another attempt by the state's humanitarian bureaucracy to usurp parental authority with substitute rules of thought and conduct.

The proportion of courses offered in American colleges that amounted to pure indoctrination and made only an occasional formal bow to knowledge has never been assessed, but it became markedly high, with only a minority of institutions managing to resist pressure, whether from within or without. But the administrators of most educational institutions toward the end of the 20th century began playing the games of disaffected students and tenured-faculty radicals. Triumphant ideologies, always guided by a determined minority, first intimidate and then roll over a weak and vacillating authority. So the vocal students and faculty members who rejected traditional education were placated.

The policy makers came to join the attack on the values the university ostensibly stood for. Like all other determined attempts to enforce literal equality, this one came down to thought control. At first only five prestigious institutions banned verbal abuse, in or outside the classroom, that was deemed sexist, racist, or homophobic, but lesser institutions quickly lined up behind them in the threat to take official action against those whose speech was declared to be offensive.

One university prohibited "misdirected laughter." At one time over 300 colleges and universities enforced forbidden speech codes, in sum a Rube Goldberg social invention. To ensure multicultural diversity, separate and segregated facilities were assigned to favored minorities. Egalitarian snobs want discrimination as a right for those historically discriminated against, in a contradictory and confused way.

No one knows how long the conditions described will persist. At the present time under challenge, egalitarian snobbery and its attendant ideologies could return in some kind of vindication, as the established ideologies of early 17th-century Britain returned with the Restoration. Any civilization is so made up of factions unable to communicate with one another that the supreme political belief of most Americans, in equal opportunity to prove what one may become, could fail to control the future.

Be that as it may, a degree of counter pressure to egalitarian snobbery appeared in late 20th century. A few brave women students argued in class that feminists had no right to assign a uniform role to all women instead of outlining the options available to them. Some heterosexuals declared they felt victimized by gay political aggression. And some white students protested the favoritism conferred upon blacks.

It was one thing to denounce a racism practiced in Pretoria, quite another when racism was defined in such a way as to deny opportunity to oneself. Students who sought admission might be told that grades and test scores were not enough to admit them lest the proper mix of students might not be achieved. If they made it past that barrier they learned that a dual grading system had been installed. Their interim reaction was a numbed acquiescence to the way things are, but they were not the only victims. There was the black recipient of a scholarship who could not write a simple declarative sentence, who might be flunked out before graduating, and also the capable young black who had to live out his life with the suspicion that he had never earned his degree.

But expressions of dissatisfaction with egalitarian snobbery failed to deter those professors and administrators who had an established stake in it. Their tacit endorsement of Thomas Hobbes's notion that ideal interests can become primary in the clash of interests created the irony of the ACLU invoking the First Amendment to protect the free expression of ideas in the classroom. In a compounding of irony, the ACLU continued to demand more affirmative action.

But we are all alike only in our basic human nature. The contrary message of egalitarian snobbery is this: we are all alike in a literal sense, and only vicious forces and institutions stand in the way of perfection. Of course the victims of those forces and institutions need the guidance of those who know what the truth is.

Meanwhile, old grads wrote enough checks to keep private higher education funded. Like them, the trustees fled from awareness. According to Irving Kristol (himself a university trustee), the trustees knew what was going on but feared to get into ideological arguments with experts in ideology. They hoped for the best.

The main issue in higher education lay beyond ideological dispute or intervention or reform. Universities could no longer produce gentlemen, nor for that matter scholars in the traditional sense. The scholar can flourish only when he is acknowledged to be a gentleman, a state of affairs which requires a class structure. The liberal arts were equipped to produce mostly indignant drones and rootless career seekers.

Back in the 1920s and 1930s that "superfluous man" Albert Jay Nock expressed scorn for a world which had no use and less respect for received ideas. Nock was what

Victorians called low-born, but he created himself into the model of gentleman and scholar. And although they had no place, in or out of the university, a few isolates strove to keep the faith, even into late 20th century. Any dependable perpetuation of the type, however, would have required a set of conditions impossible to recreate.

THE NATURE OF PREJUDICE

Prejudice is an indispensable word, something often used to castigate others for harboring it while expressing one's own prejudice. The focus of attention can also shift rapidly. Television, for example, now taunts traditionalists while a few decades ago television advised against the wiles of certain progressive causes. The family, fortunately for traditionalists, changed more rapidly on TV than in America. TV changed from a cautious agent of social control to one of unbuttoned hedonic individuation.

The bureaucrats of the mainline religious bodies made a similar conversion, in the same period of time. Official pronouncements of the mainline religious bodies, of the universities and the media—among those who control the word flow—express prejudice without apparent awareness. Older definitions of tolerance and intolerance are not currently at issue. What is instead being transmitted is a kind of innocent progressive hostility toward social order itself.

That hostility creates victims of prejudice on all sides. Much of labelled prejudice can result from fatigue and disappointment. Many suburban whites have retreated from what they once considered their social responsibilities, but at the same time they feel severe guilt because they no longer promote desegregated schools, integration and racial justice. That guilt they say has not been assuaged by their overriding fear of blacks, or by acknowledging to themselves that government programs designed to confer racial equality have not worked out.

The Three Forms of Ethnic Prejudice

Exclusionary attitudes, defined as abominable by the dominant sensibility, are in fact as necessary as they are inevitable. At the same time, as now conventionally defined there is no way to deal with prejudice, since it has been redefined to mean hatred of a persecutor for a victim. The charge of "unconscious racism," for instance, can only in reality refer to a ubiquitous phenomenon, so that what is called, below, conventional prejudice bears no intrinsic relationship to vengeful prejudice, which does express hatred.

There are three forms of prejudice: conventional, active, and vengeful. Conventional prejudice is limited to a conscious avoidance based upon a pre-judgment of what might occur. Not all of such reactions stem from misinformation; some of them represent personal experience. What of someone who correctly anticipates the racial identity of a reported mugger?

Conventionally prejudiced people can behave in ways strange to searchers for consistency, although these strange ways provide no basis for either the promotion of brotherhood or formal instruction in methods to achieve altruism. The rescuers of Jews during the Holocaust included a few people who were conventionally prejudiced against them. Without any support from other non-Jews, they nevertheless risked more than their own lives.

Even when prejudice lapses to the level of active expression, to disparagement of the selected out-group, a gap can open up with overt behavior. Joseph Epstein has written about novelist James Gould Cozzens, who in his work expressed dislike of Jews and was possibly the last famous man of letters in America to make such an unacceptable admission, that Cozzens' best friend, his only friend, his wife, was a Jew. Such rationally strange accompaniments of active prejudice appeared in 17th-century England, when isolated gentry landowners privately counted some quasi-serf as best friend. None of the people cited was making a statement of principle.

The new cult of ethnicity discloses active prejudice—as well as psychological therapy, self-flattery, and a preference for esteem over accomplishment. Although the rewriting of history in the perspective of present concerns is an old theme, the latest emphasis goes much further, openly and fraudulently rewriting history for declared ideological purpose. One black historian was hounded by his black and white peers for presenting incontrovertible evidence of black African and American complicity in the slave trade, and Egyptologists were afraid to rebut the palpably false claim that the ancient Egyptians were really black.

Vast civilizations have been discovered in the African past, when peace ruled as the alphabet and a number of other inventions appeared. Feminist historians have shown that, long before the written word, women invented spoken language, fire, and abstract thought. These discoveries reveal deep prejudices, against whites in the first instance, against men in the second.

These discoveries also exemplify active prejudice, even though only conventional prejudice is inevitable, simple pre-judgment, a perception of the world as divisible into categories, dichotomized as we and they, in- and out-group. That is the only way the world can be perceived,

The Nature of Morality

with vivid pictures of personified categories. The background of thought is an incessant social struggle, clashes of interest, official or tacit suppression, official or tacit censorship—and then unexpected results. Prejudice at the margins may be a pathological condition, but prejudice itself remains an inevitable part of social life.

In one way, all that can happen in the case of prejudice is a shifting of targets, as well as an historical waxing and waning of old ones. Perhaps the fullest expression of philo-Semitism was achieved in England and America during the 17th century. Cromwell may have lambasted the Catholics of Ireland, but he admitted Jews back into England after an earlier expulsion. The Puritans perceived the Jews to be God's first children, themselves the new Israelites, especially in America. In America's dominant Christian tradition, anti-Semitism has always been opposed.

The key question is this: How much is prejudice reduced by propaganda against it, and to what extent does a mere shifting of targets occur? Because of widely varying perceptions, ultimately idiosyncratic, such a question is difficult to address, perhaps impossible to do so convincingly. Still, the amount of hatred, name-calling, determination to smash people or at least banish them from the realm of acceptable discourse, ran much higher at the end, say, than at the middle of the 20th century. When literal equality became the highest ideal, those who tried to follow *religious* ideals, those who refused to adopt the protective coloration urged upon them by directors of emerging social standards, were marked for attack. As in- and out-groups were re-formed, the universal and safe object of prejudice became the traditionalists.

They also became the only permitted target of *vengeful* prejudice. Their children were exposed to ridicule of people like their parents every night on prime-time TV. Traditionalists, having been labeled the *common* public enemy, were not at all perceived as targets of prejudice, and could with impunity be depicted as bigots, religious kooks, hate-mongers, and dangerous subversives.

Traditionalists, in short, were denied victim status, a status which otherwise was extended to more and more people. Victims popped up with unprecedented identities. Where once, for example, there was one recognized victim of rape, another, however cautiously, was being granted favored status—the rapist. Extreme progressives designed therapy sessions for rapists, who were respectfully asked "What do *you* think should be done about this problem?" So they joined that numerical majority granted victimhood, which made hatred of traditionalists all the more essential to the progressive outlook. That the most extreme feminists accused all men of rape, even in marriage, only discloses the utter confusion of vengeful prejudice.

Vengeful Prejudice and Class

Vengeful prejudice is a substitute for the expression of class superiority, and some have argued that such enthusiasms as feminism, environmentalism, denouncing of racism and homophobia, are all religious as well. But there are differences, at least of degree. Militant feminism is a more obvious substitute for a declaration of class superiority than environmentalism. Feminists can not only avoid responsibility for several forms of self-indulgence, but also declare that I am better than you. Their attitudes of class superiority are masked by expressions of vengeful prejudice. Of course, only militant feminists, the man haters, push matters to such a logical conclusion.

They define exclusion, them and us, in a violent way.

The Nature of Morality

They can at once identify others of their own superior status—as ladies and gentlemen once could. The one certain key which enables the new egalitarian aristocrats to recognize one another is the bristling indignation they share. Unappeasable denunciations of racism and homophobia also violently define exclusion, them and us, with an attractive mask for vengeful prejudice.

RACIAL AND ETHNIC PREJUDICE

To achieve a world free of prejudice has become one of the proudest intentions of utopian thought; unfortunately, the limitations of human nature impose denial of success. All people bind with others while they reciprocally exclude at least some others. "These are my people" may make for group coherence, but that same claim implies, if it fails to state so, that those others are not my people. The drive of egalitarian snobbery, based upon a determination to eliminate prejudice among appointed villains, is thus doomed to fail, faced with extinction even while it becomes more powerful.

The drive of egalitarian snobbery is both incoherent and contradictory. Authority must always be questioned, while government authority must always force recalcitrants to obey progressive dictates. Everything that is difficult should be made easy, while anyone who fails to pass the ideological test should be reviled. The entire progressive crusade exemplifies the inevitable nature of prejudice, in its most determined and insidious form.

The way any collectivity is organized escapes reform of prejudice, since those who make the best case against it are themselves the worst offenders. Bankrupted progressive illusions have revealed, as well as exacerbated, an underlying reality. The nature of prejudice is expanded upon

Social Class and Prejudice

below in a series of brief ethnic-group and racial snapshots, not to attach blame for varying expressions of prejudice but only to demonstrate ubiquitous tendencies.

There is another caution. Traditionalist as well as progressive has been taught, for the most part, in the same schools. All educated people in late 20th century knew that there is a greater range of difference within each racial or ethnic group than there are differences from one group to another. Nor is there any need to resurrect those biological-hereditary racist arguments, impassioned refutations of which have scared off attempts to acknowledge perception of group differences. It is hoped that origins of even causes can be ignored in a simple claim that there are central tendencies of behavior, however superficial, which distinguish one large grouping from another, and that such tendencies persist in time.

Reaction by various minority groupings to this assumed fact has oftentimes been both contradictory and illogical. On one hand, they may insist that all people are alike, that anyone who admits of group differences is not only prejudiced but a bigot as well. On the other hand, they may also insist that their own group possesses special and superior qualities. Militant feminists face the same quandary when they deny all sexual differences while insisting in one way or another that women are superior to men.

There is a further complication in attempting to apply the progressive-traditionalist distinction to ethnic and racial groupings. What usually, but not always, accompanies traditionalism is a need for striving to justify self with successful effort. The last English immigrants lacked that quality, and so did rural blacks. Still, both remained traditionalist, despite a lack of drive toward stair-stepped goals. Rural blacks, however, retained traditionalism from one generation to the next, something which traditionalist urban Orientals, with their family-centered drive to succeed, could not do.

Orientals and Immigration

Oriental immigrants, the ultimate masters of the near and the particular, brought with them a fierce devotion to family and a distaste for causes, especially those people who arrived from China or Vietnam. They worked harder than any other Americans, laboriously saved money, produced children who embodied the work ethic as they labored beside their parents. These children ran ahead of everyone else at school; mastery of a new and strange language presented them with no difficulty whatsoever, unlike those dropouts who had been told that they "needed" teachers who spoke solely in whatever alien tongue. Second-generation Orientals flocked to the hard-subject courses in school, and in college where they were in some places refused admittance in order that "more representative minorities" might be favored. Most of them, nevertheless, wound up as technical professionals or independent businessmen.

They achieved a median income which exceeded that of all others, including American Jews. There were no pathologies nor did they accept any crippling government indulgence. This idyllic fulfillment of what Americans were once taught in school lasted through the second generation. Then assimilation loomed in the third, when a few Oriental youngsters organized juvenile gangs.

According to reliable reports, the third generation became more open than their parents to progressivism. Many of them no longer studied intensively, instead cultivated a social conscience. They spent more time on parties and cars and dating than at work. A very few of them even became beautiful souls.

And some of them committed suicide. A survey conducted by the United States Department of Health and Welfare Human Services pointed to the adolescent Japanese-American suicide rate as being 54 percent higher than the national average. This disparity has been attributed to an extravagant parental expectation of educational success that is virtually unique in the American experience. Young Asian Americans face a conflict between American individuation and parental concern with family pride. To add to their burden, other American youngsters, black and white, often resent having to compete with a super minority.

A very high majority of young Asian Americans did not commit suicide, in some degree only became Americanized, thereby demonstrating that more success for a second generation can make for less in the third. Aristotle was one of the first to point out that in human affairs a principle of reversibility can take over: "The excessive increase of anything often causes a reaction in the opposite direction . . ." Something, in this case opportunity, may work well, and then flounder with further increments. New peoples who at one time contribute to the common enterprise can at a later time cease to do so.

A wide range of producer immigrants built this country, but non-working consumer immigrants could accelerate decline. The Immigration Act of 1965 and all later such legislation reversed former policy, which had favored European immigration, to one of favoring immigration from those parts of the world where people yearn less to start a new American life than to take it easy and perpetuate centrifugal hatreds. Only in ancient times were large-mass sovereign aggregates maintained amidst warring tribes and clamoring racial and ethnic rivalries, by the absolute rule of a god-emperor.

The unknown future holds many possibilities. There could come a time when America admitted so many people of such a diversity that the able would stop coming here because living standards dropped as American tax policies approached those of their places of origin. Restriction of immigration may be the longer-term prospect. The notable heated debate on that issue is mainly conducted, oddly enough, among those who profess to share traditional ideology. On one side are those who hark back to the experience of their immediate forebears who strove to adapt themselves to what they found in America. Their immediate descendants avidly sought education, were raised in disciplined homes, and sought to assimilate to the values of the dominant Yankees.

Like everyone else, such people tend to generalize on the basis of personal experience. They perceive modern unrestricted immigration as a mere repetition of their own experience and that of their parents. At the same time they denounce the growing divisiveness of ethnic-group withdrawal into separation, by language and identity. They are distressed that the new immigrants are typically proud to announce that they are not Americans and do not want to become Americans.

Another camp of ideological traditionalists argue that unrestricted immigration can only, and perhaps irretrievably, change whatever is left of the American Way of Life. Politicians, meanwhile, seek to avoid immigration restriction for fear of incurring the racist label. In such a calculation, there is more to be personally gained by risking collective disaster, by endorsing the false proposition that in *unlimited* diversity lies strength.

Both sides on the issue, however, agree that with unrestricted immigration whites will shortly become a minority in "their own country." The differences among them are measured by how that prospect is viewed. Ideological traditionalists argue that immigration at the turn of the century resulted in a kind of assimilation that worked only because of the enforced pause in immigration: the earlier immigrants had to become Americans. They had no other choice available, since the immigration laws of the twenties took away the welcome mat, which was laid down again in 1965. In short, turn-of-the-century immigration worked because it was stopped. Given the sway of egalitarian snobbery, though, it is unlikely that our borders, now open to the entire world, can be closed. That bleak outlook the last wave of British immigration to this country was spared.

The Last British Wave

After the British Revolution, the hopes of radicals for redemption in this world collapsed. Empowered men of the Restoration, fearful of any threat by renewed enthusiasm, forbade enthusiasm even in the Royal Society. The suppressed working class had to settle into their own identification, with no aspirations left to direct the course of events. Later reforms, such as anti-slavery, remained concerns of the petit-bourgeois non-conformist conscience. The working-class mood lacked any vestige of revolutionary fervor, even when the French Revolution was being reported. A narrow life, with cap-in-hand when required, was accepted without the old Leveler and Digger scorn.

Before these reversions to passivity were taken, the first wave of immigration settled North America, prodded by an economic depression at home as well as by actions taken by James I against religious recalcitrants. These Puritans of rural background, yeomen for the most part, with a sprinkling of journeymen and small tradesmen, stood well above what became the working class. The last wave, in contrast, *was* working class.

These very young men, attracted by the higher wages offered in the American textile industry, came from the industrial Midlands at the turn of the century. They were not peasants, like the Poles and Southern Italians who shipped with them; they were town boys, and usually if not always left their women in the old country. They did bring a loyalty to the relatives and friends who accompanied them third-class on the Cunard Line, and these ties were never severed by the families they later formed.

After landing at Boston Harbor in ill-fitting suits, with awkward manners and bad teeth, these young men settled where familiar jobs were located and familiar people lived, in Southern New England—Manchester, Boston, Pawtucket, Fall River, New Bedford. Unlike the immigrants from Southern and Eastern Europe, they showed no interest in seeking a place in or around these cities with an adjacent plot of land to grow familiar foods. Instead they sought crowded unpaved streets with available cheap housing, such as a three-decker wooden tenement. Most of them married the immigrant women they worked among—Poles, Italians, Portuguese, or French-Canadians—stirring from one English wife mutterings about this family turning into a bloody League of Nations.

With their arrival in large numbers huge soccer stadia appeared across Southern New England, as well as pork-pie bakeries which also sold tripe and blood puddings. There were fish-and-chip restaurants, which also provided take-out orders wrapped in vinegar-soaked newspaper.

This list of familiar places did not include their own pawn shops, nor did they use the ones available here. Not only was the 60-hour week shorter than what they had done in the old country, the wages were much better.

Incredibly, they failed to bring their pubs. Fairly heavy drinking continued, but in their own homes with visiting brothers, cousins, and old-country pals. Distilled liquor, being expensive, was spooned into pint-pots of hot tea, though only on ceremonial occasions. In the earlier years they had bought ale and beer to bring home. With Prohibition, home-brew displaced them.

They retained Yorkshire and Lancashire accents intact unto death, as well as a preference for scatalogical over sexual humor, a working-class characteristic that went back to the 17th century and beyond. Neither in this country nor in England were they church-goers. The Puritan tradition had run out. Some of them, as children, had been taught to sing echoes of Puritanism at nonconformist-chapel Sunday Schools, such as "Durr t'be a Daniel/ Durr t'stand alone/ Durr t'have a purpose firm/ And durr t'make it known." At alcoholic sing-songs, Daniel and similar familiar refrains were belted out with clownish, faintly self-mocking humor.

As their ancestors for several generations had done, they turned over their paypackets to their wives, in this country usually to girls born with names hard to pronounce or ending in a vowel. Their wives in turn doled out a dollar or two for tobacco, alcohol, soccer-match admissions, and, with the higher wages of the forties and fifties, five or so dollars, some of which went for dog-track betting. She knew as well as her husband his old-country temptation to spend fecklessly that, in the absence of inner discipline, had to be curbed by someone else. As in the old country, the wife then assumed sole responsibility for running the house and raising the kids.

These men were not savers because what was an established American tradition of getting ahead was totally alien to them. These Sons of Martha rarely aspired to the place of the Sons of Mary. "It's good enough for a working man," the final judgment on housing or clothing, extended to the factory. A man allowed himself, was allowed by his pals, to become a loom-fixer, but the next step, to "second-hand" floor supervisor, was not taken for fear of the unknown, fear of being thought stuck-up, fear of attracting hostile envy. They lacked both parts of that Jewish combination of diligent free-enterprise and visionary politics. A disdain for politics may in part explain why the English workingmen played no active part in the great textile strikes of the early twenties.

Their outlook, then, combined indolence and passivity. Their extremely low divorce rate was outranked only by their non-existent police record. They produced no gangsters like the Italians nor any politicians like the Irish. They could not claim, on the other hand, any monuments, works of art, inventions, not even any immigrant-boy success stories, a circumstance which never troubled them. There was, to be sure, an occasional obscure Jude, but like most of the self-educated of that time he would follow a side path or blind alley, like Biblical prophecy, phrenology, magnetism, or atheism by way of Joseph McCabe in the 5-cent Julius Blue Books.

Such exceptions aside, these people were unwilling or unable to get ahead, as the phrase went. They waited to see what luck would bring; they worshiped not the bitch goddess but Fortuna, these believers in the Land of Cockaigne, the Big Rock Candy Mountain. They preferred a life of spontaneous gratification. A narrowed present devoted to self-indulgence consumed their interest, so that their ability to infer others' motives, intentions, expectations, remained minimal.

It was their extreme misfortune to be born too soon to enjoy the largess of the nanny state. Bismarck's Germany gave birth to it, and several British temporary acts were followed by the dole (the Act of 1920, called Unemployment Insurance) which covered all manual workers. But the dole arrived too late to keep the last wave at home.

In the late twenties some of them expressed regret at having lost that opportunity to quit working then available in the old country. If something more generous than the English dole had been offered here during the twenties, their nephews would have flocked to America like sparrows on the prevailing favorable 1921 immigration quotas and never, ever, got up early to go to work. Harry Lauder sang their song: "Oh, it's nice to get up in the morning, but it's nicer to lie in your bed."

Is any assumption about universal vanity and rivalry proved wrong by this accounting? Not at all. They were Englishmen, maybe bottom-of-the-heap Englishmen, but, by God, Englishmen. Wogs always did start at Calais, and they knew themselves to be superior to the Wogs they had settled among, even married. Envy and striving for advantage are most intensive among those who are stationed closely together. These particular non-Wogs competed for recognition among themselves, for appreciation and to ensure that no one else they knew did or had something denied to them, such as a victrola or a player-piano.

Their situation has not changed—at least in modern Britain, where a lower-class outlook still prevails. Far in excess of other Western Europeans, two-thirds of the population when questioned identify themselves as work-

The Nature of Morality

ing class, although some of them feel superior to all scruffs and scroungers, as well as to all foreigners. As in America, these non-Wogs, no matter how muted their striving may have been, by defining inferior out-groups affirmed a kind of "class" and "religious" superiority.

As for the larger sphere, and on those rare occasions when differences between British and American expectation were acknowledged, they appealed to their own version of medieval suppression. The nobs would always be nobs and workingmen would always be workingmen. They did as well as they could but they never had a chance, an alibi denied to more politically important minorities of a later day by an official insistence upon improving them.

The last wave of English immigration was protected in other ways. These men never experienced failure because failure is measured by the gap between aspiration and result. They never aspired to very much in any serious way, and they were permitted to accept themselves. Since so much of their time was devoted to the enjoyment of physical comfort, whatever identity problems they may have been troubled by—and this kind of psychobabble they were blessedly spared—could only have been trifling.

By late middle age they had seen their restaurants and bakeries converted to other use or abandoned and boarded up, their soccer stadia turned into shopping malls and parking lots. They adopted baseball, spent many hours before TV sets watching the game and many more arguing interminably about the merits of one player over another. One-time schoolboys with faulty memories of English kings could now rattle off complete statistics on every Red Sox player. And then they all died. What was the meaning of their experience? Did it add up to anything? Did history justify their existence?

Probably not, but by the same token the famous first

Social Class and Prejudice

wave had no way of knowing that they would become icons, and since their kingdom was not of this world they possibly would not have cared, because a love affair with posterity was a late 18th-century invention. Immediate posterity treated Our Forefathers casually. Those first inhabitants of Plymouth left no tombstones on Burial Hill for us to reflect upon since their grandchildren used those handy slabs for cesspool covers.

History confers or denies a respectful posterity with a roll of the dice that can be cast long after the event. The meaning of the first wave was retrospectively invented by enthusiastic 19th-century antiquarians. These people created their own larger-than-life Separatists and then ensured that the image remained solidly embedded in the schoolbooks, which it did until respectful mention of Christianity was banned in public schools.

As for the last wave, their remarkable achievement was a comradeship, unreflective and intensive, that disappeared from American life on any appreciable scale with their deaths. Beyond that, their accomplishments can best be expressed in terms of what they escaped. They were wanted, or rather their labor was wanted. They never felt that they had no place. They were never told that they were a social problem.

Much as most of them wished the case otherwise, they were not denied responsibility for their own lives. As others measured failure, they were allowed to fail and enjoy the only life they knew or wanted. They were never patronized by being told in advance of their own stupid decisions that they would be excused for making them. There was no bureaucratic pressure from their own or any other kind to get an education or to take remedial work and an unwanted job. They were never stung by a gathering impatience with their settled preference for mindless enjoyment of the present moment, nor worried about being competent to hold a job without the protection of a group quota, nor face open skepticism about their right to hold that job.

In short, they were permitted to be different from other people. All human beings, of course, are basically alike. Everyone, whether as individual or group member, can be relied upon to behave in the same basic ways. At the same time, within uniformity lies a wide range of superficial differences, for both individuals and groups. The group differences, moreover, tend to persist in time.

Persisting group differences of the last wave, though, only trace back, to the late 17th century, not forward to their descendants. They left no enduring neighborhoods or ghettos. With their deaths their way of life was gone. In this case the melting-pot worked splendidly, according to all hopes and expectations, however severe the lapse was among descendants of the Poles, Italians, Jews, Irish, and others who also arrived in large numbers at the turn of the century.

Not all was lost. There were the names, many of which had originated in ancient trades such as smith, wright, hunter, barber, tanner, miller, farmer, porter, forester, weaver, mason, bowman, baker, fuller, draper, carpenter, mercer, carter, tinker. But their children and grandchildren married into the melting-pot, so that only in the thinning male line were the names perpetuated.

The women who married their sons often converted to Protestantism, considered to be more classy, and worked on their husbands to accompany them to church. Their granddaughters-in-law drifted either way, for by this time there was a challenging chic about being Catholic, and in some cases they took their husbands to Mass. With the next generation there was no remembered ethnic tension left, and religious behavior settled at the norm of indifference more or less characteristic of the world around them.

The names became fewer but they persisted. In some cases British name married British name, thereby concealing an intervening mixture. Those who bore the names, however, no matter how acquired, and whatever their own wish in the matter, became WASPs, part of a fictive majority against which more numerous minorities, as they were called, were enjoined to organize against. They never did, though, perceive themselves as being WASPs, which was a later coinage, but as being separated from two classes of Yankees: the Swamp Yankees who preferred rural poverty to urban work, and those Yankees in the saddle who ran things and confidently represented what America was.

Even denied WASP identification, no pathos manipulation for their hitherto unclaimed victim status should be inferred. Their children and grandchildren stayed in Southern New England, and continued to work in a mill, although, as the cotton industry moved South, their children went to work in machine shops and their grandchildren into high-tech outfits. The old taboo against advancement was gone; some of their children achieved posts in local management. In any meaningful sense, and with uninterrupted prosperity since World War II, their descendants of every recent generation ceased to be working class. Some of their children spend their retirement winters far from home, playing golf in the Florida sun.

American Jews

Comprising less then three percent of the American population, Jews wield an influence that overshadows their numbers. And they share one salient characteristic with

The Nature of Morality

American Orientals, and that is loyalty and devotion to the family. They differ markedly, however, in concern about political ideology. While American Jews are traditionalists in family behavior, they tend to be the most ideologically progressive of all American groupings.

On the traditionalist side, they are disciplined and hard-working, notably concerned about the welfare of other people as well as their own. In comparative terms, the only terms available, there is not much in the way of crime or drugs or booze, and surely not divorce. The gay Jew is a startling novelty, and even heterosexual fooling around is contained.

The family is absolutely central in Jewish attention. A large majority of Jews can count on the celebrations and rituals, the shared old jokes and habits, the abiding pleasures of settled family life. Most Jews earn the assurance that when they die the few who really matter will honor them in memory. These are people of sober temperament, with a bourgeois outlook. They know that unless, God forbid, something dreadful should happen, tomorrow will be much like today.

As for their extremely progressive ideology, most Jews did not, like other successful minorities, tend to become politically traditionalist as they moved up the economic ladder. In a phrase often used, they lived bourgeois but voted Hispanic. According to Irving Kristol, communally-oriented Jews had little taste for the Anglo-Scottish-early-American tradition of Locke, Hume, and Adam Smith, so that the gathering emphasis upon political self-autonomy passed them by. Instead, they wedded their passionate commitment to social equality with expectations of universal regeneration.

While most other Americans, again according to Kristol, share a tradition of English constitutionalism, the

Social Class and Prejudice

political orientation of Jews was formed in eastern Europe, where the French Enlightenment continued uninterrupted through Marxism to form perceptions of political reality. Thus the later state of Israel could not forsake a fealty to socialist dogma amidst a disastrous economy. In America the anomaly of successful capitalists embracing visions of association with the downtrodden has persisted with like stubbornness.

In his piece "Another Look at the Jewish Vote" (*Commentary*, December 1985), conducted for the American Jewish Committee on the 1984 National Survey of American Jews, Milton Himmelfarb summarized the results as indicating an unwillingness to sacrifice for Israel, not in economic terms but in a refusal to change old voting habits. A majority wanted funds for U.S. defense curtailed, but they also wanted U.S. aid for Israel's defense expanded. They continued to vote overwhelmingly for one political party, but they also admitted that the other, on the record, had been more pro-Israel.

Of all groups and institutions in America they perceived blacks as being the most anti-Semitic, but by eleven to one they wanted to "improve relations with the black community." Finally, only one in five agreed that since fundamentalists and evangelicals ("the Christian Right") have been outstanding in their support of Israel, that Jewish objections to them should be overlooked and Jews should "work more closely with [them] to help Israel" (page 43). Himmelfarb made no effort to conceal his exasperation: And all those diplomas!

Still, account must be taken of those with memories of time past for whom the cross will always remain a hideous symbol of violent death. And yet on the other hand are American Jews now unable to distinguish hostiles from friendlies? Hollywood's producers and writers, who are predominantly Jewish, are extremely sensitive to evidence of prejudice against blacks, but according to Benjamin J. Stein, are quite unconcerned about anti-Semitism.

Do American Jews fail to define their own interests properly? That good question most individuals of any background would hesitate to apply to themselves. Right or wrong, interests are what they are perceived to be. At the same time, perceived interests can and often do have unwanted results.

The so-called foreseeable future is unknown. A reluctance to give up old allegiances is thus understandable, as well as a reluctance to forgive old rejections, because there is always the possibility that old allies, now enemies, will once again become old allies, while old enemies, who now wear what could be a mask of friendship, may revert. Such reluctance is understandable, but it remains more a feeling state than a thought. Alliances are always made or turned down on shifting ground, with no assurance of permanence.

In this case no alliance was ever really formed. There was too much envy and resentment for that, too much social distance, too great a gap in experience and imagination. Urban blacks have had experience of Jews as people in charge of them, as school teachers, social workers, landlords and shopkeepers, as their immediately known white superiors. Whether classic anti-Semitism was involved may be doubted, since a similar black animosity was aimed at Orientals who ran shops in black neighborhoods, another mockingly successful minority, this time a racial minority.

A largely self-appointed black leadership accepted accommodations around specific issues about which most blacks remained uninformed. That black leadership announced their perception of blacks as being patronized and held to impossible collective standards by a conspicuously successful minority, not, in their view, a fellow minority. This resentment did filter down. Jews became identified with impatient waiting for rapid strides once the total political emancipation, the housing, education and job training were all in place. But unlike most Jews and Orientals, most blacks, like the last wave of English immigrants, were not driven to succeed. They shared the English preference for enjoying the present moment over working at the future.

People will accept without question what they are told about the need to improve themselves only so long as they feel defenseless. At some point in a gathering control of their own circumstances they will reject those whom they come to identify as their tormenters, much as the black elites in Africa spurned the white Christian missionaries who taught them, doctored them, and in some cases fed them. No people with any awareness of what is going on really enjoy being lifted up by outsiders.

One especially persisting Jewish characteristic has been the belief in a special mission to the world, clung to by sophisticates who find quite risible any notion about a Chosen People, as in the wry joke "Dear God, please choose another people." Some outsiders nevertheless perceive a continued belief in that special mission, despite a Jewish brief against group differences of any kind. Words themselves will not, any more than stereotypes, march in a single direction: Jews simultaneously cohere and are plagued by an extreme order of internal argument, especially over what their mission should be.

WASPs, Yankees, descendants of the original settlers, whatever term may be employed, have abandoned their own mission of serving as a model to what has been called the multicultural or the pluralistic system. Jews have chosen not to replace them. A people who could do so in their basic way of life, continue to opt for a melange of political-utopian approaches to reality, some of which feature attacks on the persons and beliefs of fellow American traditionalists, especially practicing Christians, the least anti-Semitic of all non-Jews.

According to Benjamin J. Stein in his survey *The View from Sunset Boulevard* (Basic Books, 1979), the mission of the mostly Jewish TV writers and producers living in Hollywood is to displace anything and everyone they perceive as standing in their way (page 136). Their vision of America is therefore somewhat tilted. Small towns, for instance, are invariably evil and murderous. The aim of these people, says Stein, is "to take the top positions" but they realize "that other power centers must be denigrated and humiliated . . ." (page 135). Since they really do believe in conspiracy theories, they treat powerful others as their enemies, especially wealthy businessmen.

People who are perceived as playing leadership roles, such as religious figures, "are treated as bad or irrelevant, while underdog groups—the poor and criminals—are treated as deeply sympathetic" (page 127). It is "a highly parochial, idiosyncratic view of the world that comes out on TV screens, the world view of a group whose moment has come" (page 146). This world lacks tradition or restraint, folk wisdom or family heritage; it features swimming-pools and life in the fast lane.

The most acute desire of these people, according to Stein, is to lead America to their own vision of the future. Since the only life worth living is that which is unexamined, they are really not interested in the social issues they ostensibly care about (page 106). As Stein depicts these people, they are the same ravening egomaniacs Thomas Hobbes conjured up in his blackest moods.

It was since Stein wrote his book that especially scurrilous interpretations of Christian behavior have appeared with appalling frequency. One of the worst offenders, an admitted extreme example, featured a Protestant minister who supplied his wealthy businessman pals with child sex victims selected from his own rescue mission. Very few Protestant ministers know any multimillionaires, so that the inauthenticity of this script becomes at once apparent. Hollywood's continued effort, though, was ecumenical; but again, most Catholics never saw a nun gloat over the collection take.

The Jews of Hollywood seem ignorant of Murray Friedman's warning against courting powerlessness, any reckless determination to achieve splendid isolation. Jews need the stable order some of them heedlessly continue to attack. He says that too many of them believe their safety lies only in law and reason, not in any attempt to share at least part of the outlook of the Christian majority.

Christians, whatever their past record, became in the 1970s the most determined of outside supporters for the State of Israel, at a time when progressive opinion—including that expressed by some Jews—would soon begin to waver. America in the second half of the 20th century had achieved a bad record for selling out small-nation allies. Another limping Wilsonian crusade to set the world a-right had become bored with an old theme and was seeking a new one.

But the books will not balance. Moral determinism was flouted when Friedman's warning apparently went unfulfilled. So there was no necessary connection between the Hollywood treatment of Christianity and the American threat to sell out Israel. Christian parents may have been outraged at the way they were treated by the electronic media, but, except for controlled withdrawal from TV,

The Nature of Morality

they were not moved to retaliate. As has happened so often in history, an apparently inevitable clash veered off with an unexpected shift of the ground.

After decades of a shunned melting pot, toward the end of the 20th century the intermarriage rate suddenly rose to forty percent, and the matter of being Jewish ceased to have the old consequences, for Gentile and Jew alike. This development may still have been a mixed blessing, at least for Jews who retained any vestige of orthodoxy. The rising intermarriage rate does not guarantee that the residue of anti-Semitism will continue to wane. Intermarriage rates in Weimar Germany were also very high; they were soon associated with torturous Nazi definitions of precisely who was a Jew.

Even more ironically, Jewish coherence, the so-called clannishness, historically has been strong under conditions of persecution, and it has waned rapidly with casual unreflective acceptance. Old Jews may have long memories, but younger ones do not. Jews of whatever age are so characteristically imbued with rationalism, secularism, and humanism that any attempt to revive the sacred society faces powerful opposition. In short, for Orthodox American Jews casual acceptance has exacted a heavy price. Indeed, the price of additional religious indifference has been paid by Christians and Jews alike.

American Blacks

The power of perception to direct continued action into a rut of shared misunderstanding is shown by the fact that most blacks view Jews as their enemies and most Jews view blacks as their friends, perhaps reluctant but surely ultimate friends. By any statistical measure of behavior in each group, they are both wrong. But a much worse misapprehension arose about how best, in the prevailing sentiment, to "bring blacks into the mainstream," a patronizing assumption of a total control by still another "we."

One result has been to make "children of the poor" the special objects of sexual manipulation. Black children, and increasingly Hispanic as well, are deemed incapable of sexual restraint, so that the free distribution of condoms in the public school has been almost restricted to where most of them are, in New York City, San Francisco, Los Angeles, and Washington, D.C. And the floundering attempt to make youngsters feel good about themselves is as patronizing as sexual manipulation, disclosing the admission that "we" can live with the fact that black youngsters cannot learn. "Children of the poor" is code for "poverty is the basic cause of all their ills"—except that there was incredibly more poverty in Harlem during the Depression, while black crime was a fraction of what it became. Racism is another basic cause, except that each survey taken shows a sharper decline than the previous one in white racist attitudes. That very strange phenomenon, prejudice, can vary independently of disappointment over unimproved behavior.

No, it was huge and remote government programs, and the expenditure of more billions of dollars than have ever been counted, that failed to improve the behavior of the so-called urban underclass. In a classic case of unanticipated and unwanted results, that behavior steadily became more distraught: murder by their peers was the chief cause of death among young black men. Relieved of personal responsibility by their insistent saviors, who outbid with subsidies the market price for their labor, black women found making illegitimate babies a profitable enterprise while the men were returned to Thomas Hobbes's state of nature. The black urban family was virtually wiped out, destroyed by well-meaning white reformers who themselves did not understand that traditional family life, or an achievable approximation thereof, is the indispensable source of decent conduct. As one police chief summarized the mess: An "entire generation has got lost." Forty percent of all murders committed in this country involve blacks killing other blacks, while two thirds of all black births are illegitimate.

Progressive whites will do everything for American blacks except permit them to find their own way. Whatever the range of unwanted results might be, "we" know all about what is best for blacks, except to let them alone when laws are not flagrantly broken. White guilt, meet black rage. Actually, there is no evidence about how many white Americans ever shared that fashionable guilt. Most white Americans are of much more recent background than black Americans, and presumably some of them do not feel personally responsible for "the social problem of three hundred years of persecution and injustice." Possibly they share less guilt than fear of being mugged.

In the train of white progressives appeared black spokesmen who shared no interest in a common destiny with other Americans. In Joseph Epstein's words, they perfected the art of victimization by simultaneously playing at being martyr and bully—and they became rich. These were the people who insisted upon separation and created such verbal abominations as Afro-American. Much more than white progressives, they shifted political attention away from equal treatment to special treatment. They enticed the black underclass to hide behind charges of racism to protect themselves from the risks of growing opportunities, and instead to demand the protection of quotas from competition. Quotas were disguised as "new civil rights," from which Congress specifically exempted itself in all hiring for its own bailiwick, and which not at all affected the composition of Hollywood's producers and writers on the one hand, nor the fields of performing entertainment and professional athletics on the other.

Affirmative action is unattainable—only quotas and double standards are. Those standards have impelled acrimonious results across the country in law suits by white students, teachers, policemen and firemen. Blacks and Hispanics are thus stigmatized by the implication that the much lower scores they make in qualifying tests are all that is expected of them: whites would flunk with your scores, but you can pass.

Actually, this level of affirmative action causes less resentment among whites than does the favoritism conferred upon blacks and Hispanics at higher levels of employment—in law offices, government employment, the clergy, and university appointments. If less often complained about, equally resented along with the "welfare program for middle-class minorities" is the courtroom behavior of favored minorities. The total breakdown of the "trial by one's peers" fiction has proved how disunited a people we have become. Favored minorities on juries can no longer be trusted to accept the possibility that one of their own could be guilty as charged. Favored minorities as acknowledged victims have no obligation to reassure the white enemy with their behavior, because enough of the enemy will say they understand any failure on their part to behave like citizens.

Legally-enforced quotas have not evenly distributed all identified groupings throughout higher education and the workplace. The effort was surely made, even though, like many another camel's nose under the tent, the original

The Nature of Morality

Civil Rights Act of 1964 obligated the opposite of what later became law. As Thomas Sowell has pointed out, the equal opportunity of 1964 came to mean preferential treatment. In and outside of government a vast bureaucracy held onto power by "delivering perks to a constituency," a constituency not of the downtrodden but of the well-off black elites who got the "set-aside" benefits in college and at work. Meanwhile the total breakdown of the black family in the slums went unaddressed.

Employment or unemployment aside, it has yet to be demonstrated that in the absence of discrimination all ethnic and racial groups would be equally distributed throughout the division of labor. A clear majority of Americans, when they are allowed, act on their perception that capability to handle a job is the primary determinant of placement in the division of labor. This perception is never admitted in the electronic media, which continue to pick at the scabs of racism and depict contemporary blacks as beings of total competence.

In public debate, on the other hand, the possibility that certain excesses of the welfare state might be one source of an acknowledged black underclass was admitted to discussion. But the possibility was never entertained that if blacks should be perceived not as victims, instead as citizens responsible for their own choices, that a way out of some dilemmas might form. Any start in that direction, however, would require changes almost beyond probability, such as a renunciation of attempts to impose equal results and a return to fostering the ideal (never a wholly achievable goal) of equal opportunity. A start in that direction, although implausible, is the only move which could lead to a reconstitution of the black family in the urban setting.

Can that goal be achieved? Both major parties, taking the next rhetorical step, have denounced "dependency on welfare" and promised that welfare mothers may have only a limited number of illegitimate babies, beyond which all welfare payments will be cut off. Such manipulation is designed to make traditionalists feel good, but no one will adopt such a plan. What about the courts and constitutional guarantees? What about the humanitarian backlash of punishing innocent babies? How can so-called crack mothers be taught discipline and self-reliance by government, especially by a government which endorses the charge that white racism is the cause of black pathologies?

One goal which many people of both races once professed, an unselfconscious acceptance of one another, has receded with the white insistence upon defining, and creating, blacks as a "social problem." Only an individual blessed with formidable talent and stamina can surmount the dreadful handicap of that perception. Blacks are indeed victims, in a way untouched by the progressive imagination. Unlike Orientals, blacks are officially discouraged from accepting menial jobs, so that only a determined few can get started.

Brotherhood never was a reasonable prospect, for there is none of that across white ethnic groups. A shared existence, without hatred and fear, is on the other hand something to which very few would refuse to subscribe. Such would doubtless be a tarnished goal, although surely an improvement over the conditions which seemed to be at least temporarily set for perpetuation in late 20th century. Sadly enough, intentions at best only fitfully affect the massive changes which occur in the big picture.

American blacks are faced by a dilemma very similar to that of Eastern Europeans. Should they continue to drift with the ideology of equal treatment for all in-group members, or opt for individual achievement and thus insure that many of them won't make it? The terms of

The Nature of Morality

that answer will require payment in emotional terms that outweigh material considerations. American blacks would have to eschew the protection of blaming racism for all the deficiencies and limitations of individuals among them. This is not a collective choice: it is one only individuals can make.

But even if greater numbers of blacks should escape blaming racism for all of their own deficiencies, the path will be rocky for any individual who pursues the American Dream. He may have to dress with meticulous care in order to improve his chances of getting the cab he intends to hail. On the job, he may be mistaken for a messenger. No matter how hard he works, how can he ever prove that he is not a token black nor escape the suspicion that he may be the beneficiary of affirmative action? He may be perceived with either ignorance or hostility, or what is worse, he may have to put up with uneasy whites who are trying to prove their own lack of prejudice. Still, if he is patient and lucky, he may even discover potential friends.

INEVITABILITY OF PREJUDICE

Throughout most of the 20th century the basic operating public assumption had been the wisdom, the inevitability, of association. Old identities would fuse in Jean de Crevecoeur's new race of Americans. In short, assimilation would triumph. Then that theme suddenly shifted to one of preserving differences and distinctions, to the justification of righteous confrontation in the black case, and to collective boasting about exclusionary pride up and down the ethnic scale.

It was no longer clear what an American was, mainly because any model to measure one's self against had vanished. Newly assertive centrifugal interests replaced older centripetal assumptions. That this new shift violated a companion insistence—upon the literal equality of all peoples so that group differences do not exist—went ignored. The new shift *did* succeed in exacerbating underlying tensions, as delusion was indulged by ideological progressives in their own writing of the revised script.

Mindless and self-destructive rage in the black case was justified, as well as hyphenated Americanism among the rest of the numerical majority. These moves were accompanied by a legally-directed horror for spoken as well as written denigration of any favored people, be they blacks, feminists, or homosexuals. If need be, total fabrication was endorsed in such aims, as in the equivocal minority status assigned to Asians who, in some newspapers, have been called "Anglos," have been lumped together with equally fictitious "Anglos." Only those who vie for government help in large numbers, Native Americans, Hispanics, and blacks, qualify without reservation for approval.

As has been demonstrated above, there is no way to eliminate prejudice. There never was, in any century. The essential difference between recent past and present time is the growing reluctance to acknowledge, or even grasp, the essential place of repression and suppression in setting limits to a freedom now defined, by the people who control the word-flow, as unlimited individuation, unlimited aspiration, unlimited choice, unlimited license.

No utopia looms as a result of all this effort. Specifically, the total amount of prejudice encouraged as well as expressed has not at all decreased; it has increased. What Plato warned about, that democracy can become a maddened beast on the point of rending itself, appears to be in prospect—for the short term. Human nature is so volatile, however, that all kinds of alternatives to the transitory present are not only conceivable but inevitable. Perceptions of reality can, will, readily shift.

At the same time, what has persisted is a faith in government to order things to be the way they should be. From one era to another that faith has shifted in intensity, but, given a challenge most citizens feel incapable of handling by themselves, that faith once again waxes. The danger of repeating unremembered history is part of very few calculations.

Given the breakdown of consensus (with one result being a vast increase of prejudice), the state as problem-solver is turned to more often than previously. The breakdown of consensus also ensures that unanticipated and unwanted consequences of state action will mount—again, for at least an interim period. One reason why unwanted consequences proliferate through state action is the widespread and touching faith that "government" must (or should) be a protecting entity which hovers over all citizens to make certain that justice is ultimately done. Justice is never achieved, unless in someone else's definition. Each person, white, black, Hispanic, or whatever, is consumed by his own perceived interests, at times at subliminal levels, where the warmth of collective prejudice against outsiders can dominate consciousness. For any given individual, justice is never far removed from some modicum of self-vindication.

The State

There is no government that "cares" for its people, that seeks to confer justice upon its faceless charges; there is only a fragmented collocation of organizations, each with its own rules and purposes, which require each part of it

Social Class and Prejudice

to hide behind his organization. IRS hacks have been told to get the money; whatever tactics must be employed will be covered by the organization. Any attempt by the taxpayer to find out what is going on runs into the cover-up, whereby no one can be held responsible since each worker knows about only a small part of the total assessment. Politicians, though, can be trusted—by their pals in either party. The farther any individual is in ability to threaten the interest of at least one politician, the more he might be advised to depend upon himself to solve his own problems.

In short, the political process is slippery. Minorities of power always rule, no matter what the official designation of the government, in part because human nature is so volatile that logical opposites can be happily, and unpredictably, embraced within a short period of time. President Franklin D. Roosevelt, for example, promised preelection voters that he would reduce taxes, the budget, and welfare cost. Instead the voters got the New Deal and the Brain Trust, which took charge of their lives. Envy of the rich and eager acceptance of dependency replaced traditional citizenship enough to usher in an icon worship hitherto unknown in American life. In many immigrant homes the picture of the Madonna over the sofa was replaced with that of the new savior.

Later, the money ran out, and no real intensification of the old reversal could occur. Innovation became more equivocal. Present-day governments, with their politicians going in various directions, as well as entrenched bureaucrats fulfilling their own perceived interests, come up with diverse solutions to argument and pressure. The solution offered in one place invariably falls athwart what other government people are proposing.

The Surgeon General and people in other bureaus make

life miserable for American smokers while the Department of Agriculture subsidizes the sale of tobacco products in foreign countries. Some bureaus are busy imposing new regulations while other bureaus are equally busy trying to reduce the unwanted consequences of old ones. Again, while one politician stresses the need of government support for "family values," another who represents a big-city constituency advocates public-school condom distribution without parental knowledge.

Several bureaus and progressive lobbies press to "make guns illegal." Laws were once passed to ban all cheap hand-guns, so that importation of them was effectively banned. The domestic market was thus encouraged, so that the "inner city" was bountifully supplied. The Gun Control Act passed by Congress proved to be ineffective in a world where who has a right to do what becomes negotiable as well as controversial.

Traditionalists tend to approve of punishment for criminals, since they assume that only suppression of crime will work. In one way or another, progressives stress the responsibility of non-criminals to remove the basic, the root causes of crime. Federal and state bureaucrats and politicians equivocate, by trying to satisfy both sides, so they go along with plea bargaining to reduce the number of criminals who must be punished. Meanwhile they play out the charade of punishment, in part by getting right with the construction unions, who inflate the cost of prison construction and thereby reduce the possibility of punishment.

Whatever politicians and governmental functionaries of divided organizations might do, they do not pay the cost of crime; only the victims of crime do that. The non-criminals of the inner city may beg for the incarceration of

Social Class and Prejudice

criminals, but what do they know? The one thing the state will not do for them is protect them in their own streets.

The state cannot "solve" any other than technical problems. Multiculturalism, for example, the idea that any way of life is equal to, or perhaps better than, any other, cannot be legislated. Members of various minority groups (in total they far outstrip the number of Yankees) are now engaged in a power struggle to prove who has been most victimized and whose claim of superiority in the past should displace all others. They must sell their own argument not only to white progressives but to competing minorities as well. But the only place where the exclusionary dickering can be settled is the marketplace of interests, not that of ideas.

Although exclusionary dickering may be a kind of substitute for the standards of responsibility claimed by social classes, government cannot settle whose delusions about past glories shall prevail. It has tried, as in the government task force on Native American Education which advocated back-to-the-blanket (over the decades the Bureau of Indian Affairs has alternated between encouraging young Indians to leave the reservation and join the mainstream, and to go back-to-the-blanket). The Task Force urged a "multicultural environment" to promote tribal languages and culture, despite, or perhaps because, the American Indian high-school dropout rate is higher than that of any other racial or ethnic group—so back-to-the-blanket. The proclaimed idea of multiculturalism is to raise self-esteem, an insecure condition that requires emotional isolation and encourages jockeying for official handouts. And that kind of self-esteem will not raise achievement levels, since multiculturalism did not do that for black youngsters, for whom it was originally devised.

Here is a clear example of intervention by the state

resulting in exacerbation of racial and ethnic prejudice. Each labeled minority seeks to prove that its own victimization in the past is more clear than any other, and therefore it is entitled to supreme recompense from the state. One minority is set against another in this conflict over claims for special and exclusive favors. The basis of morality, a combination of family, religion, and social class, is only weakened by such self-righteous demand for attention. All elements of morality are consciously or inadvertently undermined by the state—manned as it is by fractionated organizations and by people who can afford to think only in terms of personal short-term advantage.

INDEX

Abortion, 39–40, 71, 99–103
Africa, 5–6, 119, 145
American Separatists, 138–139
Aristotle, 131
Authority, 116–117

Barzun, Jacques, 114
Becker, Carl, 106–107
Benedict, Ruth, 61
Bible, 48, 74, 111
Blacks, 144–145, 148–154
Boas, Franz, 59–60
Boulding, Kenneth E., 10, 11
Bradley, General Omar, 115–116

Christianity, 78, 85–86, 89–92, 107–112, 147
Christian Schools, 67–72, 73, 76
Civil Rights Act of 1964, 151–152
Cleaver, Eldridge, 120
Comte, Auguste, 85–86
Cooley, Charles H., 15–16, 17–24
Cozzens, James Gould, 125
Crevecoeur, Jean de, 154
Crime, 8, 158–159
Culture, 29–30, 60–61, 62, 68

Darwin, Charles, 28–29
Deconstructionism, 118–119
Division of Labor, 32, 152
Durkheim, Emile, 65, 91

Electronic Media, 44, 73–74, 102, 123, 143–144, 146–147, 152
English Immigrants, 133–141
Enlightenment, 106–107, 143
Epstein, Joseph, 125, 150

Fallacy of Contextual Choice, 5–6
Family, 63–67, 77–78, 79–81
Feminism, 34, 37–43, 127–128
Fletcher, Joseph, 108–109
Freeman, Derek, 56, 57–58
Freud, Sigmund, 28, 30, 56–57

Giddings, Franklin H., 60
Golden, Harry, 64–65

Hedonism, 77
Higher Education, 113–123
Himmelfarb, Milton, 143
History, 11, 43, 54, 111–112, 121, 125, 132, 138–139, 144, 148, 150
Human Nature, 4, 8–9, 11, 14–15, 21, 24, 54, 66, 87, 104, 111–112, 122, 128, 137, 155–156, 157
Huxley, Aldous, 6, 62

Idealization, 43, 44, 107, 120
Immigration, 130, 133, 190

Index

Immigration Act of 1965, 131, 133
Inclusion-Exclusion, 20, 24–26, 30–33, 79–80, 86, 96, 124, 126
Interests, 20, 27–28, 117, 122, 144, 154–155, 156, 157, 159

Jews, 64, 89–92, 124, 141–148
Judges, 7, 97, 99

Kinsey Studies, 36
Kristol, Irving, 122, 142–143

Leisure and Entertainment, 75
Lewis, Bernard, 119
Lewis, C. S., 54–55
Lewisohn, Ludwig, 61
Lippmann, Walter, 2

MacIver, Robert M., 16–17
Marriage, 33–36, 49–50
Marshall, General S. L. A., 10
Marxism, 106, 118–119, 143
Maslow, Abraham H., 25–26
Mead, George Herbert, 18–19, 21, 22, 28
Mead, Margaret, 4, 40, 54–63, 92
Methodological Dilemma, 23–24
Modern Gnosticism, 37, 105–112
Moral Behavior, 18, 19, 22, 34, 37–38, 70, 74, 80–81, 88, 91, 94, 107, 160
Multiculturalism, 120–123, 159

Neuhaus, Richard J., 103–104
Nock, Albert J., 122–123

Oliner, Samuel P. and Pearl M., 89–92
Orientals, 130–131

Parsons, Talcott, 16, 22, 93–94
Paul (St.), 11
Perception, 10–12, 13–14, 101–102, 126, 148–149

Plato, 33, 155
Politicians, 3–4, 9, 41, 97, 132, 157
Pornography, 40, 56–57, 96–99
Prejudice, 1–2, 24, 52, 63, 93, 113–123, 123–156
Psychologist's Error, 5–6
Public Schools, 64–65

Reality, 9–12
Reik, Theodor, 36
Relativism, 23, 51–55, 84–85, 109–112
Religion, 87–92, 94, 104, 107–112
Roosevelt, Franklin D., 157
Rousseau, Jean Jacques, 25, 34
Rules, 8, 31, 53
Russia, 53, 59

Santayana, George, 46–47, 114
Self, Private, 20
Senator Hubert Humphreys, 13
Sex, 35–36, 37
Shakespeare, 38
Social Class, 24, 32–33, 38–39, 83–86, 87–92, 113–123
Socialization, 27–30
Social Pathologies, 72–75
Social Problems, 95–96
Social Workers, 7–8
Sorokin, Pitirim A., 68
Sowell, Thomas, 152
State, 33, 35, 65, 66, 68, 69, 71, 74, 77, 153, 155, 156–160
Stein, Benjamin J., 143–144, 146–148
Stereotyping, 2–4, 6–9, 63
Suppression, 25–26, 95, 96, 138
Symbolic Interactionism, 16, 27

Thomas, W. I., 16
Tillich, Paul, 111
Tocqueville, 83, 86, 114–115
Traditionalists and Progressives,

Index

6–7, 11, 12–15, 71–72, 84, 85, 91, 95, 100, 101, 103, 126–127, 128–129
Traits and Attitudes, 19
Trust, 46–49, 55, 66, 157

Unemployment Insurance Act of 1920, 137
Utopia, 56, 83, 128

Unwanted Results, 53–54, 98, 149–150, 156, 158

Values, 51–53, 71

Waller, Willard, 35–36, 46
Weber, Max, 16, 75
Wilson, Edward O., 66, 92–93